DIVERSITY

NICHOLAS FITNESS

NELSON
CENGAGE Learning

Australia • Brazil • Japan • Korea • Mexico • Singapore • Spain • United Kingdom • United States

Diversity
1st Edition
Nicholas Fitness

Cover designer: Cheryl Smith, Macarn Design
Text designer: Cheryl Smith, Macarn Design
Production controller: Siew Han Ong

Any URLs contained in this publication were checked for currency during the production process. Note, however, that the publisher cannot vouch for the ongoing currency of URLs.

Acknowledgements
Shutterstock:
Pages 5, 6, 7, 13, 21, 23, 24, 26, 27, 28, 30, 31, 33, 34, 35, 38, 39, 40, 48, 51, 52, 53, 54, 55, 57, 58, 59, 60, 61, 62, 63, 67, 71, 79, 86, 88, 90, 92-93, 95, back cover.

Other:
Page 5, 'Sauvages de la Mer Pacifique', panels 11-20 of woodblock printed wallpaper designed by Jean-Gabriel Charvet and manufactured by Joseph Dufour et Cie; page 11, Voyage au Pôle Sud et dans l'Océanie sur les corvettes L'Astrolabe et La Zélée, Jules Dumont d'Urville, Gide Paris, 1846: Barnet Burns (from his book); pages 31, 62 Waiheke High School; page 41, NZ Church Missionary Society; page 45, A close-up view of the Za'atri camp in Jordan for Syrian refugees as seen on July 18, 2013, from a helicopter carrying U.S. Secretary of State John Kerry and Jordanian Foreign Minister Nasser Judeh. [State Department photo/ Public Domain]; page 55, Tuterei Karewa of the Ngatimaru tribe, North Island, New Zealand, Arthur James Iles (1870 - 1943); page 56, A Samoan tattooist (left), Tufuga ta tatau and assistant (right), carrying out a traditional tatau on a man's back. The tattooist uses traditional tools. Thomas Andrew (1855 -1939); page 65, Human Rights Commission.

National Library:
Pages 8-9, King, Marcus, 1891-1983. King, Marcus, 1891-1983 :[The signing of the Treaty of Waitangi, February 6th, 1840]. 1938.. Ref: G-821-2. Alexander Turnbull Library, Wellington, New Zealand. http://natlib.govt.nz/records/22308135; page 13, Augustus Earle, Alexander Turnbull Library; (Reference No. PUBL-0015-09); page 14, Louis Auguste de Sainson (b. 1801); James Cook. Line engraving by O. Birrell after H. Dodd, 1785; page 15 Zoffany, The death of Captain James Cook, 14 February 1779; Bartenwal, Zeichnung un 1870; Men killing fur seals, 1890s; page 17, King, Marcus, 1891-1983. [King, Marcus] 1891-1977 :[Reconstruction of the signing of the Treaty of Waitangi. ca 1950?]. Ref: NON-ATL-0173. Alexander Turnbull Library, Wellington, New Zealand; pages 36-37, Tempsky, Gustavus Ferdinand von, 1828-1868. [Tempsky, Gustavus Ferdinand von] 1828-1868 : [Encampment of Chute's forces near Te Putahi Pa, on the Whenuakura River, 7 January 1866 / G.F.von Tempsky] [1866]. Ref: A-198-008. Alexander Turnbull Library, Wellington, New Zealand; page 42, John Blomfield, 1905. Alexander Turnbull Library. A-315-3-042; page 43, Ana Likio at her home in Waitangirua, surrounded by luggage - Photograph taken by Ray Pigney. Further negatives of the Evening Post newspaper. Ref: EP/1991/1614/10. Alexander Turnbull Library, Wellington, New Zealand.

NZ Herald:
Back cover; pages 32, 67-68, 76, 77, 78, 82-83, 87.

For product information and technology assistance,
in Australia call **1300 790 853**;
in New Zealand call **0800 449 725**

For permission to use material from this text or product, please email **aust.permissions@cengage.com**

National Library of New Zealand Cataloguing-in-Publication Data
A catalogue record for this book is available from the National Library of New Zealand

978 0 17036811 7

Cengage Learning Australia
Level 7, 80 Dorcas Street
South Melbourne, Victoria Australia 3205

Cengage Learning New Zealand
Unit 4B Rosedale Office Park
331 Rosedale Road, Albany, North Shore 0632, NZ

For learning solutions, visit **cengage.co.nz**

Printed in Australia by Ligare Pty Limited.
2 3 4 5 6 7 8 21 20 19 18 17

CONTENTS

KEY SKILLS

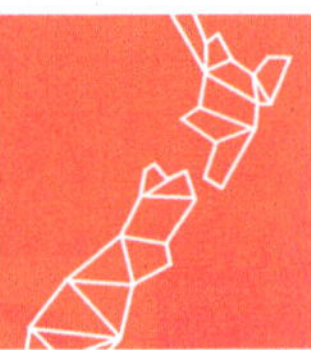

Skill 1: Writing a Paragraph

A paragraph is a logical, ordered way of communicating your understanding of a topic that you have been studying. There are three parts to a paragraph. 'TIE' is a simple way to remember the three parts.
TIE stands for Topic, Information and Example.

- *Topic* — a general statement about the topic of the paragraph.
- *Information* — expanding the topic statement by giving more information.
- *Example* — evidence that backs up what you are saying. This could be facts, a quote or a statistic.

For example, read the paragraph below about the early Polynesian explorers.

The early Polynesian explorers were the first group to discover the islands of New Zealand. (*T — Topic.*) **T**

Many islands throughout Polynesia had already been settled. However, New Zealand was further away and harder to get to. The early Polynesians that settled in New Zealand were the ancestors of the Māori. (*I — Information.*) **I**

The early Polynesian explorers used large double-hulled canoes to voyage across the vast Pacific Ocean. They arrived in New Zealand between 800 CE and 1250 CE. (*E — Example.*) **E**

ISBN: 9780170368117

Skill 2: Taking Notes

Learning how to write useful notes is a very valuable skill to develop. It involves writing a summary of a big piece of text or writing in manageable key points and phrases that you can easily remember. The purpose of taking notes is to summarise information. You can do this by underlining, or highlighting information that you think is important and then rewriting the key points.

Tips for effective note-taking:

1. Read the paragraph slowly and try to understand what the paragraph is about.
2. Read the paragraph again, this time underlining or highlighting what the main points are.
3. Make sure to write down any words that you don't understand. It is important to look up the definitions of words that you don't understand.
4. Rewrite the information that you have underlined or highlighted using short sentences. Make sure you do this in your own words. If you just copy it out you won't understand it as well.
5. Do not take TOO MANY notes – if you do, you will find it more difficult at revision time.

Skill 3: Understanding Graphs

Graph interpretation is a very important skill. There are many different types of graphs. These include line graphs, bar graphs and pie charts. Graphs present statistical information in a visual way to make the data easy and quick to understand. Graphs can be used to show how something has *changed* over time. They may also show how things are *related*.

Depending on what type of data you have will help you decide which type of graph is best to use. Five simples rules for graphing (Remember 'TASKD!'):

- **T**itle
- **A**xes
- **S**cale
- **K**ey (or labels)
- **D**ata is accurate!

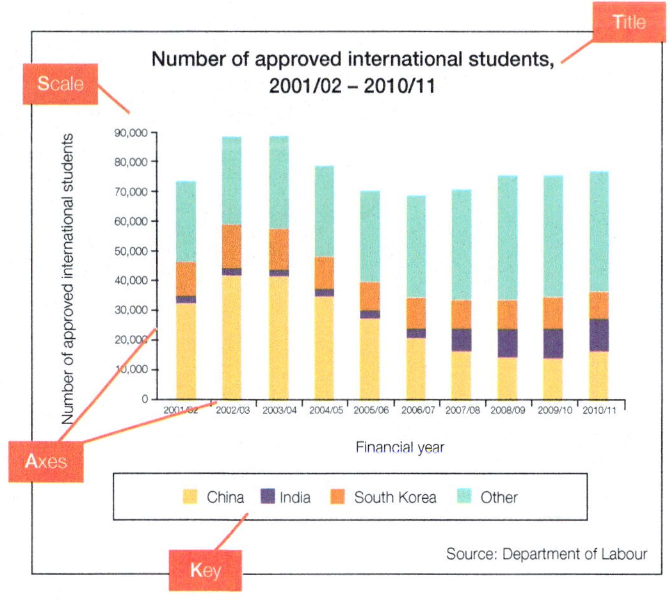

Try to get as much practice as you can at graph interpretation. The more graphs that you see and get to interpret will help you get better at this skill.

Your teacher might give you some data to practise constructing a bar graph or a line graph.

Skill 4: Drawing a Pie Chart

A pie chart is a type of graph that uses 'pie slices' to visualize information and data. To draw a pie chart, we need to represent each part of the data as a proportion of 360, because there are 360 degrees in a circle.

Example:
A survey was done at a high school to see what the most popular sport is. The results were:

Football	57%
Rugby	19%
Swimming	12%
Netball	12%

When we want to draw a pie chart we need to rewrite the percentages for each sport into degrees of a circle. To find out the number of degrees for each section in the graph we multiply the percentage by 360°.

Football 57%: $0.57 \times 360° = 205.2°$
Rugby 19%: $0.19 \times 360° = 68.4°$
Swimming 12%: $0.12 \times 360° = 43.2°$
Netball 12%: $0.12 \times 360° = 43.2°$

Now we can create the pie chart using a protractor.

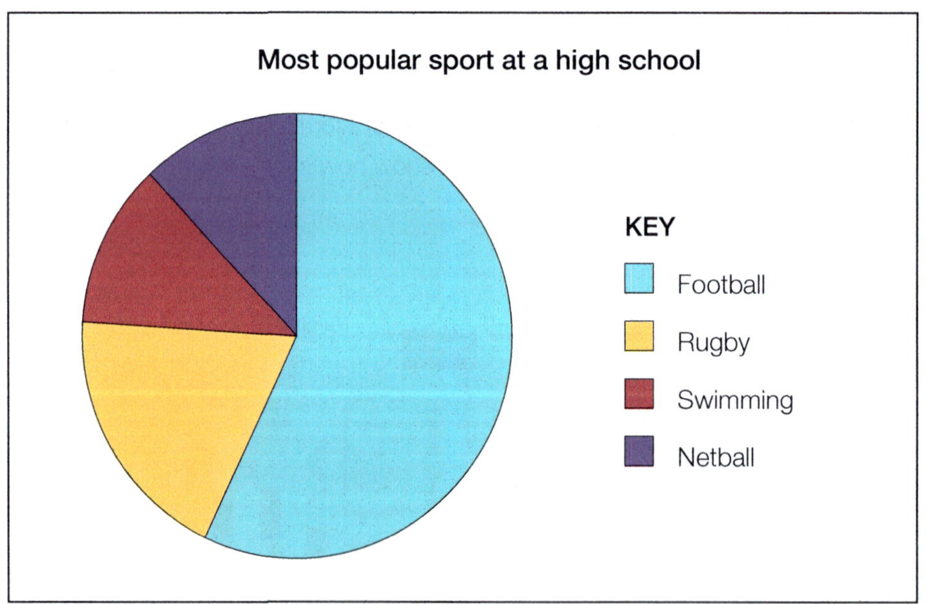

ISBN: 9780170368117

Skill 5: Interpreting Sources

Interpreting primary and secondary sources

There are many ways that we can learn about the past. These might include our own personal experiences, oral histories from family members, the work done by historians, and stories. Sources are a great way of making sense of the past. There are two types of sources – primary and secondary.

Primary sources

Primary sources are sources *from* the time. This means that they were created at the same time as the event that they describe or refer to. Some examples of primary sources are:

- Photographs
- Letters
- Speeches
- Newspapers
- Posters
- Diaries

One group of people who use primary sources for research are historians. Historians must take care with how they interpret primary sources. What might be some of the potential problems with primary sources for historians?

Secondary sources

Secondary sources are sources that are produced *after* the time of an event. They are second-hand accounts of events from the past. It is important to be able to tell the difference between a primary source and a secondary source. Some examples of secondary sources are:

- School textbooks
- Books by historians
- Internet sites
- Film documentaries

Skill 6: Using the Internet – Beware!

The internet is an extraordinary resource for gaining access to information. It has made researching a topic easier than ever before. Because anyone can create a web page, sources on the internet can be <u>unreliable</u>, <u>biased</u>, or <u>inaccurate</u>. For these reasons don't believe everything you read on the internet.

Some ways around this are:

- try to find out who is the author of the material
- check if the website has been updated recently
- use more than one website.

SO HOW DID WE GET HERE?

We are all one people. 'He iwi tahi tātou'.

— William Hobson, the first Governor of New Zealand

Learning intentions

After studying this chapter you should understand that:

- early Polynesian and British migrations to New Zealand have continuing significance for tangata whenua and communities
- the movement of people affects cultural diversity and interaction in New Zealand.

Useful words

immigration — when a person or group enters a country to live permanently.

Polynesia — a region of the Pacific Ocean (see the map in this chapter to find out which countries are included in this region)

Māori — an indigenous or native person of Aotearoa New Zealand.

fleet — a large group of boats travelling together.

pā — a fortified Māori village.

tangata whenua — native people of the land.

bicultural society — a society made up of two cultural groups.

tauiwi — means 'strange tribe' or 'foreign race', people different to the Māori.

abundant — available in large quantities.

taonga — a cultural treasure.

generation — people who are born at about the same time.

Pākehā — a New Zealander of European origin.

refugee — a person forced to flee their homeland because of war, persecution, violence or a natural disaster.

orphan — a child who has lost both parents.

multicultural society — a society made up of many cultural groups.

isolated — far away and difficult to get to.

Activity

Independent

1 Copy the chart below. Fill in the first two columns of the KWL (Know, Want, Learned) chart based on the topic: *The discovery and early settlement of New Zealand*. Then continue with this first part of the chapter. Come back to this chart and fill in the final column with what you have learned about the discovery and settlement of New Zealand by the early Polynesians and British settlers.

What do you already (K)NOW?	What do you (W)ANT to know?	What have you (L)EARNED?

 ISBN: 9780170368117

First arrivals: the discovery and settlement of New Zealand by the early Polynesians

New Zealand is a 'country of immigrants'. This is because New Zealand has had a long history of **immigration**. Aotearoa New Zealand was the last part of **Polynesia** to be settled by humans. This makes New Zealand one of the youngest countries in the world.

There have been many 'waves' or groups of immigrants since New Zealand was first discovered. The early Polynesians, who were the ancestors of the **Māori**, discovered and settled in New Zealand somewhere between 800 CE and 1250 CE.

Just like the later immigrants to New Zealand, the ancestors of the Māori arrived in 'waves'. Great ocean-voyaging double-hulled canoes left the islands of Polynesia in **fleets**. Once landings were made on the coasts of both the North and South Islands of New Zealand, some of these canoes would then return back to Polynesia to repeat the journey many times.

The date when New Zealand was first settled is an ongoing debate for historians and archaeologists. There are many different methods that are used by historians and archaeologists to try to work out a precise date for when the early Polynesians first arrived. These include:

- genealogical dating
- radiocarbon dating
- pollen analysis
- kiore (Pacific rat) bones and rat DNA.

Did you know?

People often refer to dates as 'BC' or 'AD'. These terms mean 'before Christ' (BC) and 'anno Domini' (AD), which is Latin for 'the year of our Lord'. Today, Christ is not recognised by a number of different religions and cultural groups. The terms BCE (before the Common Era) and CE (Common Era) are now more accepted. For example, 2016 CE is the same as AD 2016.

Activities

Independent

2 What are some of the reasons for why there is not a precise date for when the early Polynesians first arrived in New Zealand?

3 Research ONE of the dating methods that historians and archeologists use and write one paragraph explaining how it works. Go to page 4 and read Skill 1: Writing a Paragraph.

ISBN: 9780170368117

Activities

Independent

4 Refer to the map below and complete the following questions.

a What three regions are highlighted on this map?

b What ocean are these three regions in?

c For each region, make a list of all the islands included in the region.

d What region is New Zealand in?

e Why do you think Australia is not a part of one of these regions?

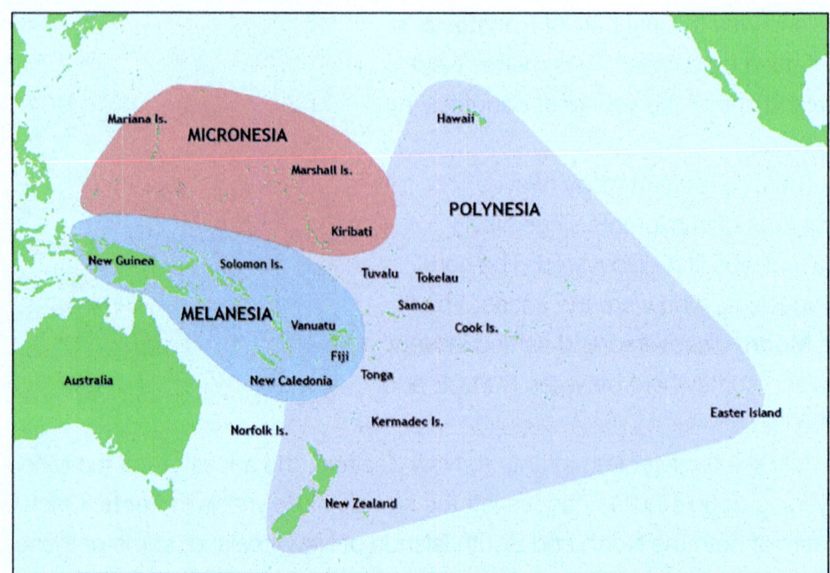

5 Refer to the map below and complete the following questions.

a What does this map show?

b What are the names of the first islands in the Pacific Ocean that were discovered?

c Approximately how long ago were these first islands discovered?

d Which continent did these people first come from?

e When was Hawaii discovered?

f When was Rapa Nui discovered?

g What is another name for Rapa Nui?

h What part of the Pacific Ocean is New Zealand located in?

i According to this map, when was New Zealand discovered?

j Construct a brief timeline displaying the information in this map.

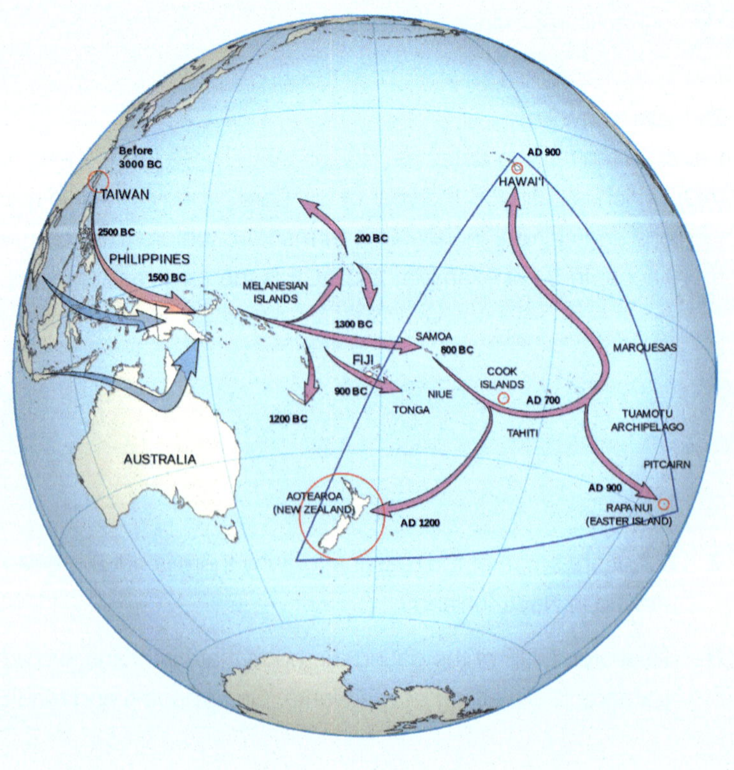

ISBN: 9780170368117

Activities

Pair

6 How might the islands of the Pacific have been discovered?

7 Why did it take people so long to discover the islands of New Zealand?

8 What are some reasons why the early Polynesians might have left their island homes to come to New Zealand?

9 What would have happened if the early Polynesians had never discovered New Zealand? Come up with three possible scenarios.

10 Write a statement on what you have learned about the discovery and settlement of New Zealand by the early Polynesians.

Extra for experts

11 Do some extra reading on the Māori myth of Kupe and the arrival to Aotearoa of the seven canoes of the 'Great Fleet'. Then come up with six questions using the 5 Ws and 1 H. Draw these balloons into your book and fill each balloon with your question. For example, one question using the W of 'Who' could be: Who was Kupe?

Once you have filled in all of the balloons, answer your questions. For example: Who was Kupe? According to Māori mythology, Kupe was a great chief who was the first Polynesian explorer to discover the islands of New Zealand.

The Māori introduced animals such as the dog and the *kiore* (Pacific rat). They also brought with them vegetables such as kumara, taro, gourd and yam.

Activity

Independent

12 Visit your local supermarket. How many of these vegetables can you still find today?

ISBN: 9780170368117

Māori lived in **pā** and worked communally. Māori were warriors and tribes engaged in warfare with other tribes regularly. The Musket Wars killed thousands and many more became slaves and refugees. Māori also developed arts and crafts and were skilled performers, storytellers, carvers, toolmakers and weavers.

Did you know?

The word 'Māori' originally meant 'the local people', or 'the original people'. With the arrival of Europeans, the word Māori gradually became an adjective for the 'Māori people'. This change took place in the early 1800s.

Extra for experts

13 Find out about the Musket Wars that were fought throughout New Zealand in the early 1800s. Write one paragraph summarising the event.

European exploration into the Pacific

Due to New Zealand's geographic isolation, several centuries passed after the arrival of the early Polynesians before the next phase of migration occurred. This was the arrival of Europeans. Before the arrival of Europeans, the Māori, the **tangata whenua** of New Zealand, had existed as a single culture of people. When Europeans arrived, New Zealand became a **bicultural** society. These later immigrants were called **tauiwi**.

James Cook.

Portuguese and Spanish ships began voyaging into the Pacific in the 1500s. However, it wasn't until 1642 CE that the Dutch explorer Abel Tasman sighted New Zealand. He was the first-known European to discover New Zealand. It was soon after this that a Dutch map-maker gave the islands the name 'Nieuw Zeeland'. Incredibly, it was not for another 127 years until the next-known European explorer, the Englishman, Captain James Cook, reached New Zealand in 1769 CE aboard the *Endeavour*. After exploring and mapping New Zealand, Captain Cook returned to England and wrote about the **abundant** natural resources of New Zealand. These resources included flax, whales, seals, timber as well as suitable soil for growing crops. Cook made two more trips back to New Zealand, in 1773 CE and 1777 CE.

Cook took back to England not just samples of plants but also many **taonga** that he had received in New Zealand. The taonga Cook took

 ISBN: 9780170368117

back to England were an important part of Māori culture from the 18th century. You can still see some of these treasures today in museums in Britain. Others have been returned to New Zealand and are stored at Te Papa Tongarewa (Museum of New Zealand) in Wellington. The Te Papa collection includes plant cuttings, carvings and cloaks up to 300 years old. Some of the tools and weapons are even older, as they had already been handed down through **generations** of Māori before Cook took possession of them.

Activities

Independent

14 Captain Cook was killed somewhere in the Pacific. Find out where and why.

15 Go to the Te Papa Tongarewa (Museum of New Zealand) website. Find some of the early Māori objects in their online museum collection called Taonga Māori. Write down what they are and where they have come from.

Cook's discovery of New Zealand led to several other explorers, many of them French, to come and explore New Zealand. Early arrivals to New Zealand from the 1770s onwards included **sealers**, **whalers**, **traders**, **missionaries** and **merchants**. The first encounters between Pākehā and local Māori tribes were mixed. Some encounters were peaceful, as both groups were very keen to trade, while other interactions ended in violence and bloodshed. Māori initially welcomed Pākehā because of the opportunities to trade.

ISBN: 9780170368117

Activities

Pair

16 Trade was a key part of the early relationship that developed between Māori and Pākehā. A T-chart is a great way to organise information. Make a T-chart of all of the goods that the Pākehā traded with the Māori (left column) and what Māori had to trade in return (right column).

Example of a T-chart.

17 Research TWO of the following groups that came to New Zealand:

— sealers
— whalers
— traders
— missionaries
— merchants.

(If you are working with a partner, you could each do ONE group.)

Go to page 5 and read Skill 2: Taking Notes. Take notes from books or the internet. Write one paragraph for each group explaining who they were, where they were from, why they came to New Zealand and examples of any interaction that they had with local Māori tribes.

18 Go back to the KWL chart at the start of this chapter. You can now fill in the final column for what you have learned so far.

Pākehā-Māori

In the first half of the 19th century (1800 CE – 1850 CE), some Pākehā, mostly escaped convicts and sailors, started living with Māori tribes. Some even married Māori women. These Pākehā men adopted Māori ways of life and became known as Pākehā-Māori. One example was a man named Barnet Burns, who was even tattooed in the traditional Māori style. He learned to speak Māori and is most likely one of the first bicultural New Zealanders.

 ISBN: 9780170368117

The Treaty of Waitangi: a turning point

In 1840 CE, there were only 2000 Pākehā living in New Zealand. The Māori population at this time was around 80,000. The Treaty of Waitangi (Te Tiriti o Waitangi), signed by over 500 Māori chiefs in 1840 CE, made New Zealand a colony of the British Empire. British immigrants now had legal rights as citizens and could come and live in New Zealand. Following the signing of the Treaty of Waitangi, mass immigration to New Zealand from Britain began.

The sea voyage was long and difficult. It took months in cold and leaky wooden sailing ships. Severe seasickness was common. When the British settlers finally did arrive, they had little contact with family back home in Britain.

Population figures for Europeans 1800–58

Year	Population	Notes
1800	50	Approximated numbers as there was no official census (counting of the population)
1815	200	
1839	1000	
1841	5000	
1843	11,489	
1850	22,000	Begins to equal the Maori population
1851	26,207	First official census
1858	59,413	

Activities

Independent

19 Picture dictation – Coming to New Zealand!

Draw eight boxes – make sure the boxes are big enough to draw a picture in each. There are eight statements below. For each statement, draw a simple picture (using no words or numbers) to illustrate each statement.

When you have completed the picture dictation, retell your story to each other in pairs.

Statements:

1 My family decided to leave Britain to start a new life.
2 My father paid the New Zealand Company agent for the ticket.
3 We waved goodbye to our friends and relatives.
4 Once we had set sail, many of those on board suffered from seasickness.
5 Living conditions were cramped and there were even live animals on board.
6 Food and water rations were limited.
7 We tried to overcome boredom by searching the horizon for land.
8 Finally, after many months at sea, we arrived in New Zealand to start our new life.

ISBN: 9780170368117

Extra for experts

20 Describe how the Treaty of Waitangi led to the beginning of organised settlement in New Zealand. Try to write two or three paragraphs.

Culture shock

Culture shock is a very real experience that people feel when they travel extensively or move to another country. It is caused by everything being different and unfamiliar — the weather, language, food, music, and so on. Once a person has become used to the new culture and embraced it, then the culture shock will fade away.

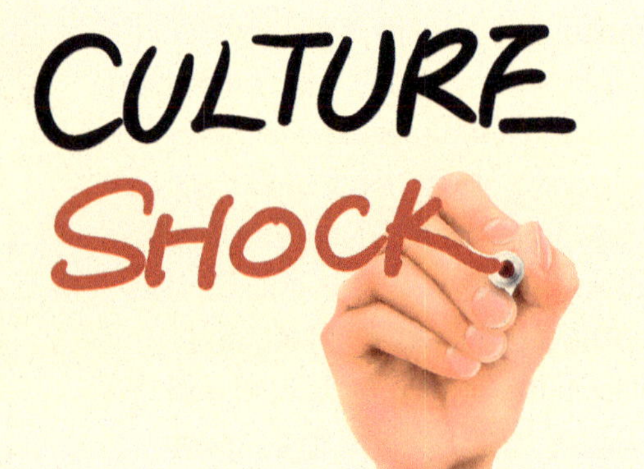

The following are the main 'waves' of tauiwi that migrated to New Zealand. The 'waves' have been put onto a timeline. A timeline is a chronological order of events, that is, from the oldest event to the most recent event.

Immigration timeline

1790 CE – 1839 CE

Groups of sealers, whalers, traders, missionaries and merchants start to arrive.

1840 CE – 1859 CE

British (English, Scottish, Welsh and Irish) settlers, assisted by the New Zealand Company, and a few small groups of French and Germans immigrate to New Zealand.

1860 CE – 1869 CE

Gold is discovered. Chinese immigrants arrive quickly in the South Island for the gold rush (some Americans and Australians came for the gold rush too).

1870 CE – 1879 CE

Germans and Scandinavians (mostly from Norway and Sweden) arrive.

ISBN: 9780170368117

1940 CE – 1949 CE

European **refugees** and **orphans** arrive in New Zealand after World War Two.

1950 CE – 1959 CE

New Zealand receives Dutch and Hungarian immigrants and refugees.

1960 CE – 1969 CE

Pacific Islanders (from Samoa, Tonga, Tokelau, Niue, Cook Islands) migrate to New Zealand.

1970 CE – 1979 CE

War refugees from Laos, Vietnam and Cambodia flee to New Zealand from South-East Asia.

1980 CE – 1999 CE

Political crises in multiple regions around the world including North Africa, the Middle East and the Balkans bring in refugees from Iran, Iraq, Somalia, Bosnia and Kosovo. Coups in Fiji caused many Fijian Indians to come to New Zealand. Following the *Immigration Act 1987* becoming a law, which favoured skilled migrants, there was a big surge in arrivals from many countries including China, India, Japan, Korea, Singapore, Malaysia, Indonesia, the Philippines, Sri Lanka and South Africa, and smaller numbers from Pakistan and Bangladesh.

Fun fact: Net migration averaged 5000 people a year, every year, between 1900 CE and 2000 CE!

2000 CE – present

There has been a steady arrival of immigrants from around the world as New Zealand becomes a **multicultural and culturally diverse society**. Demand for residence in New Zealand remains strong.

Activities

Independent

21 Search for the Immigration Act 1987 of New Zealand on the internet. Write down the FIVE most important facts about it.

22 Make a list of all the cultural groups included in the immigration timeline.

23 Using the immigration timeline on pages 18–19, annotate a world map. Draw lines for when and from where major groups of immigrants came to New Zealand.

Why do people migrate?

Individuals and groups have migrated around the world from their home countries for thousands of years. The main factor for why people usually migrate is to improve their lives. There is a range of *push factors* and *pull factors* happening.

Push factors are the reasons why people leave a particular region or country.

Pull factors are the reasons why people move to a new region or country.

Activity

Pair

24 Below are a number of push and pull factors all jumbled up. Create a T-chart and write out each factor under the heading of 'Push factor' or 'Pull factor'.

- population pressure
- poverty
- better services
- crop failure
- more fertile land
- lack of services
- political stability
- higher employment
- drought
- more wealth
- flooding
- safer, less crime
- high crime
- good climate
- war
- lack of safety
- future prospects
- lower risk from natural hazards

Immigration occurs due to a combination of *push* and *pull* factors. This migration impacts on both the place and people left behind, and on the new place and culture where immigrants settle. As New Zealand is geographically **isolated**, the immigrants who settled in New Zealand in the past must have had a strong desire to want to come here.

Nowadays there are a lot of different reasons why people want to come to New Zealand. Immigration New Zealand puts migrants into different categories. Some of these categories are:

- Temporary labour migrants
- Business migrants
- Asylum seekers ('spontaneous refugees')
- Return migrants.
- Long-term skilled migrants
- Refugees
- Family members

Activities

Independent

25 Write a statement on what you have learned about *push* and *pull* factors.

26 Write out a definition for each of the following words: **immigration**, **emigration**, **migration**.

Group

Discussion: practise *listening* to the other person talk and then take your turn to *articulate* what you think.

27 Do family life and relationships always change when families move to a new country?

28 Is it possible to stay the same in a new country?

 ISBN: 9780170368117

CHAPTER 1

Extra for experts

29 Investigate where people who leave New Zealand go to. What part of their New Zealand cultural identity stays with them when they go to a new country?

Extra for experts

30 Immigration New Zealand is planning to create a two-tier system, which will favour wealthy immigrants over poorer immigrants who speak little or no English. State your opinion on this current issue. Back up your opinion by explaining why you hold this view.

Independent

31 Learning about another cultural group in New Zealand. Select one cultural group from the immigration timeline. Choose one that interests you or maybe one that you don't know much about, and answer the questions below. Resources may be found by looking up 'New Zealand Peoples' at http://www.teara.govt.nz.

You can then:

- present your findings of your chosen cultural group to the class in an oral presentation, *or*
- create a poster or digital presentation (PowerPoint, Prezi or Google Slides, for example), which includes the answers to your questions. Include a range of images of your chosen cultural group.

a *When* did this cultural group come to New Zealand?

b *Why* did this cultural group come to New Zealand?

c What have been some *barriers* to cultural interaction that this cultural group might have faced in New Zealand?

d What have been some *positive* and *negative* consequences of cultural interaction for this cultural group?

e How has this cultural group contributed to the development of New Zealand's identity as a *multicultural and culturally diverse society*?

Time to recap

1 What is the most significant thing you have learned in this chapter? Why?

2 'The Muddiest Point'. Write down which part of this chapter was difficult to understand. Compare what you wrote down with someone else. Find someone in the class who can explain it to you.

2

AND WHAT IS CULTURE?

'The question of our essential identity is one we are still posing of ourselves. It may be many more years before we have a definitive answer. Suffice to say that we are a blend of many people.'

— Former Governor-General of New Zealand, Anand Satyanand

DIVERSITY

Learning intentions

After studying this chapter you should understand that:

- the ideas and actions of people in the past have had a significant impact on people's lives
- people remember and record the past in different ways.

Useful words

culture — the customs, beliefs and values of a particular society or group of people.

diversity — means difference and variation. New Zealand is *diverse*, which means that we have a wide range of people from different cultures, religions, beliefs and traditions.

tikanga — traditions, practices and beliefs.

unique — means the only one of its kind.

race — a person or group's physical characteristics.

ethnicity — the national and cultural background of a person or group of people.

misconception — a view or opinion that is incorrect.

cultural group — a group of people that identifies with the same culture.

cultural heritage — heritage that includes things from the past such as artefacts and traditions.

artefact — an object (for example, a tool) from the past that tells something about the culture that created it.

identity — who or what a person is, the thing that makes that person what he or she is.

whakapapa — genealogical links.

ambiguous — open to more than one interpretation.

subculture — a group of people who make themselves different from mainstream society in some way.

What is culture?

The word **culture** can mean different things to different people. The concept of culture is in a constant state of being defined and redefined. In the box below is a list of different statements of what the word 'culture' means to different people.

Statements on culture

- Culture is shared.
- Culture is learned.
- Culture does not just mean race or ethnicity.
- Culture is passed from one generation to the next generation using language and art.
- Culture is not static. It's not something we can simply put in a museum.
- Culture affects behaviour.
- Culture belongs to people.
- Our culture is our **tikanga**.
- Culture is dynamic and changing.
- A group's culture is what makes them **unique** and reflects what that group thinks is valuable and different.
- Cultural rights are an integral part of human rights.

ISBN: 9780170368117

Activity

Group

1 *Think, pair, share!*

Read through all of the statements on culture and then choose one to complete the following activity.

Think: Write down the statement on culture that you chose. Then around it, using arrows, write down all of the things that you think of when you read it again.

Pair: Discuss the statement on culture you chose with the person next to you. Let them share their statement with you. Discuss why the word 'culture' can mean so many different things to different people.

Share: In groups of three or four, come up with a definition of culture. You might have a chance to read out your group's definition to the class. The class can then choose the best definition of culture. You could use this definition as you work through the rest of *Diversity*.

Don't label me!

Nowadays more and more people of mixed ethnicity are resisting old cultural labels. The term *hapa* refers to a person who has mixed ethnic heritage. For example, Tiger Woods, a professional golfer, has made it clear to the media that he does not like being called African-American. He prefers the new cultural label 'Cablinasian', a term that combines his Caucasian, Black, American-Indian and Asian ethnic background.

Activities

Independent

2 Do you think that the trend of new cultural labels is likely to continue to grow as cultural diversity increases? Why?

Pair

3 PMI – Plus, Minus, Interesting. Try to write down THREE of each.

a What are the positive (**P**lus) things about new cultural labels?

b What are the negative (**M**inus) things about new cultural labels?

c What is **I**nteresting about new cultural labels?

Extra for experts

4 Would you describe your cultural identity as being multiracial, or do you see yourself as belonging to a single racial group? Why?

ISBN: 9780170368117

What is cultural diversity?

The term *cultural diversity* is continually expanding, just as the meaning of culture is also changing. However, there is no single agreed-upon definition for what cultural diversity means. We are all different, so cultural diversity includes everyone. **Race** and **ethnicity** are two ways of distinguishing one person or group from another. Cultural diversity can cause a wide range of positives and negatives (see Chapter 3: Cultures Collide).

There are a number of myths and **misconceptions** that surround the term *cultural diversity.* These include:

- Cultural diversity is only about minorities.
- Cultural diversity is only about women.
- Cultural diversity is something that we should worry about.
- Cultural diversity is new.

Activities

Class

Discuss the folllowing:

5 Should we always treat everybody the same and ignore differences?

6 Are there any situations in which we should treat people differently?

7 How can we develop a greater awareness of cultural diversity in the area in which we live and go to school?

8 Ask at least 10 students *that are not* in your class to complete the following sentence:
Cultural diversity is …
Record their responses and write one paragraph describing the *similarities* and *differences* in their responses.

Having a cultural identity

Individuals and groups might identify themselves as New Zealanders in some situations and as part of a particular **cultural group** (for example, Māori, Chinese or Scottish) in other situations. People might also identify with more than one cultural group. The cultural identity of an individual or group of people can be seen in many different ways. These can include:

- language
- religion
- beliefs and values
- cultural heritage sites
- sports and games
- performing and visual arts
- clothes
- music
- housing
- food
- festivals
- education.

ISBN: 9780170368117

Activity

Independent

9 There are 12 different ways above that people express their cultural identity. Write each of these down and next to each concept draw a simple picture to illustrate each aspect.

Technological advances have led to the creation of a *global village*, according to the Canadian author Marshall McLuhan. It also shows how culturally diverse the world has become.

My identity – what makes me me?

Your cultural identity affects the way you think and behave. It affects the way you relate to other people who might be from your own culture or from a different culture. A strong cultural identity can contribute to your overall wellbeing.

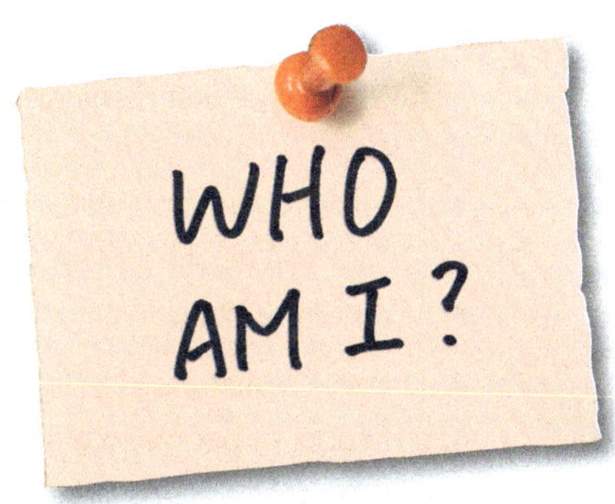

Activities

Independent

10 Draw up a family tree like the one pictured. Include siblings, parents/guardians and grandparents. You might even be able to write down the names of your great-grandparents.

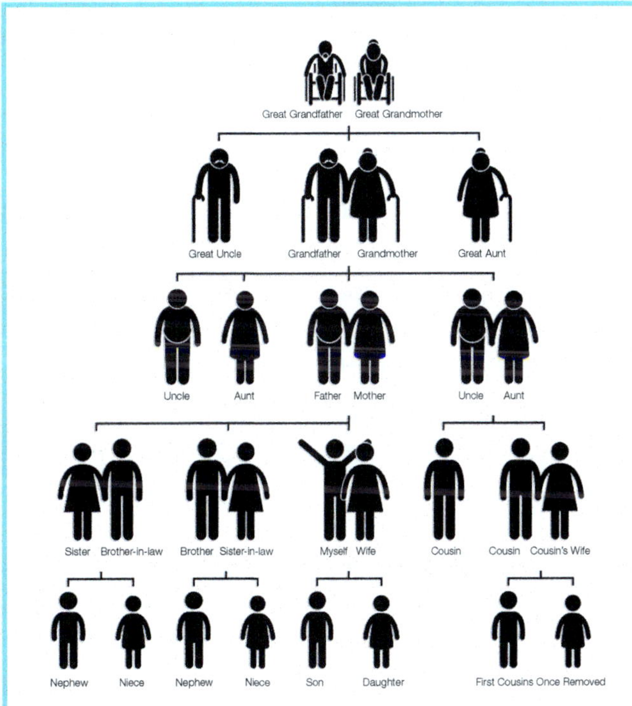

Pair

11 Put it in a spaceship!

Signals have been received from outer space. The United Nations has decided to send back, in a special spaceship, information about human life. Your task is to choose what should be sent in the spaceship (for example, photos, items of clothing, music/waiata, literature or religious objects).

In your group, brainstorm as many things as you can think of which should be included in the spaceship and write them down.

Independent

12 Make a digital presentation (PowerPoint, Prezi or Google Slides, for example) of your cultural identity. Use at least six of the aspects below. Include images, illustrations and text to accompany each aspect.

- A special family event.
- How birthdays are celebrated.
- An important festival celebrated in your culture.
- A story, myth or legend from your family.
- Sports that you play or love to watch.
- Where your first name or surname has come from.
- The language spoken at home.
- A special family artefact (an heirloom or taonga).
- Your favourite books, computer games, music or movies.

13 A survey is a useful way of collecting information. A survey involves a list of questions that are asked of a number of people to gather their views and opinions.

Complete a class survey about cultural identity by asking the following questions of students in your class:

- What is your family name?
- Do you know what country your family name originally comes from?
- When did your family first come to New Zealand?
- Where did they come from? (Locate all the countries on a world map.)
- Why did your family come to New Zealand?
- What cultures are you made up of?
- What is the most important aspect of your identity?

14 Once you have completed your class survey above, do the following. (Refer to Skill 3: Understanding Graphs on page 5.)

a Construct a bar graph of countries of origin of students in your class using the class survey data.

b Comment on the cultural diversity of your class by using evidence from your bar graph. Do you think the diversity of your class makes it more interesting to be in? Or does it make it more difficult to work together?

Extra for experts

15 **a** How does identity develop? Which aspects of identity are determined by the society in which we live, versus those that are inherent and fixed?

b How much are people judged by their individual identity or by the group to which they belong?

c Archbishop Desmond Tutu famously said that South Africa is a 'rainbow nation'. Explain what this term means. Is New Zealand also a 'rainbow nation'? Would another term be more appropriate, for example, a 'melting pot' or a 'cultural kaleidoscope'?

 ISBN: 9780170368117

Activities

Group

16 Class debate

How it works:

a Divide the class into two teams — affirmative (supporting) and negative (not supporting) on the topic.

b Each team then divides into three small groups. Each group is assigned the role of one of the three speakers in the debate. The group can decide who will be the speaker.

c Talk about the topic as a class. Brainstorm key terms and major subheadings and allocate these to each speaker. (This is to ensure that the speakers don't cover the same points.)

d Each group then prepares their side of the debate.

e Talk about debating protocol (for example, no yelling out during the debate while the speaker is speaking).

f Hold the debate! Your teacher is the judge unless you can get a special guest to judge.

Topic for the debate: **People have the freedom to choose their own identity.**

You could try to repeat this activity for a different topic.

Pair

17 Complete the following questions.

a Is it possible for someone to belong to several different cultural groups? Give some examples.

b Do you have to be born into a cultural group to understand the culture? Explain.

c If someone belongs to several different cultural groups, what are some ways that he or she might determine his or her primary culture?

d Are there instances when a discussion on culture or cultural heritage might be difficult for a person (for example, being adopted)? Come up with several different examples.

Oral histories

People remember and record the past in different ways. An oral history refers to the stories that an ordinary person tells about an event or time that he or she lived through. Oral histories are another way to learn about the past. Most of the world's cultures have evolved and passed on their knowledge and values to succeeding generations solely by word of mouth, relying on human memory alone. This information can be lost when the person dies, if it has not been written down. Historians nowadays interview older people to find out about the past and record their oral history. It is vitally important to keep oral traditions alive in order to maintain a cultural identity.

Activities

Pair

18 Complete the following. (Refer to Skill 5: Interpreting Sources on page 7.)

a In your own words, define what a primary source is.

b What are three examples of primary sources?

c In your own words, define what a secondary source is.

d What are three examples of a secondary source?

19 Pretend that you are carrying out an interview with a person who is going to tell you stories from their culture and their past. Put together a list of good interview manners that you would make sure you used.

ISBN: 9780170368117

DIVERSITY

Whakapapa

In most cultures, information about family members is passed on from one generation to the next. This is because people are proud of their ancestors and it gives them a sense of belonging. If someone asks you in te reo Māori the question 'Nō whea koe?' or 'Ko wai koe?', they are not asking you for your name — they want to know about your **whakapapa** and significant places to you.

Māori trace their ancestors through their whakapapa. This is used to describe their genealogy and trace their family tree. Whakapapa is transmitted orally and is made up of stories, waiata and traditions that tell a story of ancestry.

Activities

Independent

20 A pepeha is a way to introduce yourself in te reo Māori. Complete the following. Your teacher will help you with this.

Ko ____________ te maunga. (*The mountain that I affiliate to is ____________*)
Ko ____________ te awa/roto/moana. (*The river/lake/sea that I affiliate to is ____________*)
Ko ____________ te waka. (*The waka that I affiliate to is ____________*)
Ko ____________ tōku tipuna. (*My (founding) ancestor is ____________*)
Ko ____________ tōku iwi. (*My tribe is ____________*)
Ko ____________ tōku hapū. (*My sub-tribe is ____________*)
Ko ____________ tōku marae. (*My marae is ____________*)
Nō ____________ ahau. (*I am from ____________*)
Ko ____________ rāua ko ____________ ōku mātua. (*My parents are ____________ and ____________*)
Ko ____________ tōku ingoa. (*My name is ____________*)

Extra for experts

21 You can also try to make a digital pepeha. Record yourself saying your pepeha out loud and make it into a short video with music and accompanying pictures.

Class

22 Ask your teacher to go to YouTube and listen to New Zealand musician Stan Walker singing the 2014 song 'Aotearoa', written to celebrate Māori Language Week. The first part of the song is Stan Walker giving his own pepeha.

 ISBN: 9780170368117

Finding our place in the world

One of the most powerful Māori concepts is that of **tūrangawaewae**. This word means 'a place to stand' and refers to a place that you feel a special connection to. It might be your home, a church or a special family place.

Activities

Independent

23 Complete the following questions.

- a Where is your tūrangawaewae?
- b What are your rights and responsibilities to your tūrangawaewae?
- c Are there any symbols that identify this special place?
- d Why is it important to have a place that you belong to?

24 Write a statement on what you have learned about cultural identity.

Group

25 Features of different cultural identities.

- a **Pākehā cultural identity**. Brainstorm or make a list of all of the key features of New Zealand or Pākehā cultural identity. Three examples have been given to get you started:
  - DIY (Do It Yourself) attitude
  - Asking someone to 'bring a plate'
  - Eating foods such as pavolva and kiwifruit.

- b Repeat this for **Māori cultural identity**. Three examples have been given to get you started:
  - Having a hangi
  - Festivities for Matariki (Māori New Year)
  - Importance of te reo Māori.

- c Different cultures also have many of their own unique features, which highlight their cultural identity. Choose another cultural group and complete the same activity above for key features of that culture's identity.

Extra for experts

26 a Does New Zealand create a feeling of belonging for immigrants? Explain.

b What are different ways that Māori culture is maintained in Aotearoa today? Some examples could be kōhanga reo programmes and performing the haka before sports games.

ISBN: 9780170368117

Subcultures

When we think about culture, we often think about ethnic cultures, but there are many different types of cultures. For example, different generations have their own subcultures. Different groups in society also have their own cultures.

In New Zealand there is a large and diverse range of **subcultures** that exist. It could be through their beliefs, the way they dress, what they do, the way they talk or the music they listen to. They may be regional or local, for example the café culture in the main New Zealand cities of Auckland and Wellington. It may be gang related, for example, the Hells Angels motorcycle gang or Black Power. It may be the beach culture, for example, surfers at St Clair Beach in Dunedin or Piha in West Auckland. Or, it may be the gaming culture for those who like to play popular games such as Minecraft or League of Legends and attend conventions such as the annual Armageddon expo in Auckland.

Activity

Pair

27 What does the 'baby-boomer' generation refer to? What are some of the issues New Zealand has started to face due to having an ageing population?

Café culture

One firmly established subculture that exists in New Zealand is a 'café culture' that has developed in recent decades. It has become an important part of the city pride of many of New Zealand's cities.

Activities

Pair

28 Write down all of the subcultures that you can think of, and categorise them. For example, two subcultures you might choose to write down is the Christian community of Gloriavale on the West Coast of the South Island and the Destiny Church movement. These two subcultures would fit under the category of 'Religious subcultures'.

Independent

29 Write a statement on what you have learned about subcultures.

  ISBN: 9780170368117

National identity

New Zealand is a diverse nation, made up of many different cultures and subcultures. A national identity reflects people's understanding of who they are in relation to others. For example, some people might understand New Zealand's identity by looking at New Zealand's history or at famous New Zealanders' sporting and artistic achievements. New Zealand historians have pointed to key events in our nation's history that have helped to create a national identity. These include:

- women granted the right to vote in 1893
- formation of ANZACs in Gallipoli, Turkey in 1915
- New Zealand becomes nuclear free in 1987.

Others might see it by looking at our national symbols and icons. Māori culture may form one aspect of a New Zealand national identity, since it is both unique to New Zealand and a part of our identity in the outside world. Even though New Zealand has a small population, New Zealanders view themselves as strong, courageous and independently-minded. This shows in our passion for extreme sports and mountaineering. It is also evident in our obsession with the national sport, rugby. New Zealanders are proud of our 'clean and green' environment and an open and equal society.

The term 'New Zealander' is a very *ambiguous* term, as over 200 different ethnic groups now call New Zealand home.

Activity

Independent

30 **a** Design a bumper sticker to advertise New Zealand to the world.

b Imagine that a tourist travelling around New Zealand asked you for the FIVE best things to see and do. What would you say were the FIVE best things and why?

ISBN: 9780170368117

For you, being a New Zealander might mean that you are proud when our national sporting teams, such as the All Blacks, Black Caps or Silver Ferns, play well against another nation. It might also mean that you feel a sense of pride and belonging when you hear the national anthem being played. You might also have negative feelings when someone criticises New Zealand or thinks that we are a part of Australia.

Activities

Pair

31 A typical New Zealander!

Choose someone in your class. Draw up a T-chart. On the left side of the chart list ALL of things that make them a typical New Zealander. On the right side of the chart list ALL of the things that do NOT make them a typical New Zealander. Make an overall statement, using your T-chart, on whether or not you think that they are a typical New Zealander.

Independent

32 The New Zealand national anthem.

Research some information on the current New Zealand national anthem, and then complete the following.

- **a** What is the current national anthem of New Zealand called?
- **b** What anthem did it replace in New Zealand?
- **c** In what year was it first sung?
- **d** Write out the words of the two verses.
- **e** What does the phrase 'Pacific's triple star' in the English verse refer to?

Group

33 Brainstorm or make a list of all of the key features of a New Zealand *national identity*. Three examples have been given to get you started:

- Our founding document, the Treaty of Waitangi.
- Famous birds such as the kiwi, tūi or kererū.
- TV programmes such as *Shortland Street*.

The kiwi bird is so closely associated with New Zealand that people from other cultures often refer to New Zealanders simply as Kiwis!

The great New Zealand national flag debate

Find an image of the current New Zealand national flag. Find an image of other flags of New Zealand such as the tino rangatiratanga flag or the 1835 Declaration of Independence flag. Name two other countries that have changed their national flag. What do you think about changing the New Zealand national flag for a new flag? Come up with a design for a 'new' New Zealand national flag.

 ISBN: 9780170368117

Activity 

Independent

34 Your local shopping centre: a mini-inquiry.

If you were to take a walk around your local shopping centre, you might see evidence of the cultural diversity that exists in New Zealand. Carry out a mini-inquiry at your local shopping centre. This will require you to visit your local shopping centre at least once. Complete the following.

a What is the name of your local shopping centre/shops and where is it located?

b Record the names of all of the shops and the services that they offer.

c Record details of any signage at your local shopping centre.

d Ask the shop owners if they are happy for you to walk around the shop and note down any evidence of the types of goods that they sell, for example, taro sold at The Happy Vege shop, *The Mandarin Pages* sold at the East Street dairy.

e Using evidence collected from your mini-inquiry, do you agree or disagree with the following statement? (Provide justification for your response.)

The shops, services, signs and types of goods sold at my local shopping centre reflect the cultural diversity of my local community.

Time to recap 

1 What is the most significant thing you have learned in this chapter? Why?

2 'The Muddiest Point'. Write down which part of this chapter was difficult to understand. Compare what you wrote down with someone else. Find someone in the class who can explain it to you.

ISBN: 9780170368117

3

CULTURES COLLIDE

'Celebrate diversity, practise acceptance and may we all choose peaceful options to conflict.'

— Donzella Michele Malone, American author

Learning intentions

After studying this chapter you should understand that:

- cultural interaction impacts on cultures and societies.

Useful words

acculturation – exchanges of cultural features with foreign cultures. This word sometimes appears as 'enculturation'.

generalisation – making a general statement that applies to many people but not necessarily all.

desegregation – elimination of segregation.

racism – hatred or intolerance of another race or culture.

fatal impact – refers to the devastating effect that the arrival of Europeans had on Māori.

intermarriage – marriage between two individuals of different cultural groups.

prejudice – (a feeling) a negative or hostile attitude or opinion towards a race or group of people formed without sufficient knowledge.

discrimination – (an action) treating a person or group of people differently based on their religion, race or culture.

scapegoat – an individual or group that is made to take the blame.

derogatory – showing a lack of respect for someone or something.

stereotype – (an idea) an oversimplified generalisation about an entire group of people without regard for individual rerekētanga (differences).

perspective – a particular attitude or point of view about something.

When cultures first meet

Cultural interaction occurs when two or more cultures meet for the first time. This process of cultural change as a result of contact with another culture is called **acculturation**. The positive and negative effects of cultural interaction can be seen at two levels:

- the *group* level, for example, changes to clothes, food and language
- the *individual* level, for example, changes to daily behaviour.

DIVERSITY

 ISBN: 9780170368117

Activity

Class

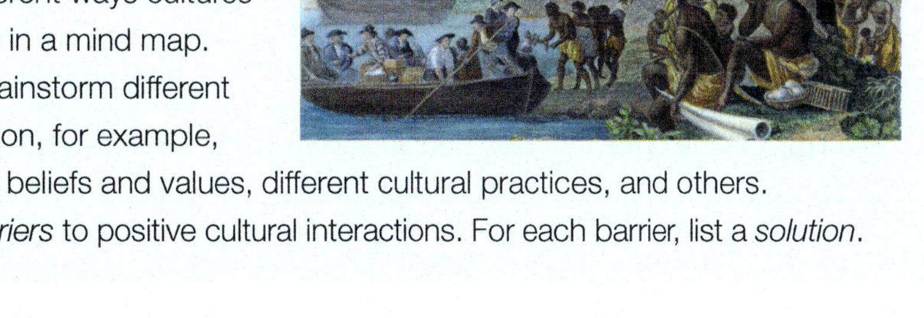

1 What factors influence the nature of cultural interaction?

   a Make a list of all of the different ways cultures can interact. Record these in a mind map.

   b As a class, discuss and brainstorm different barriers to cultural interaction, for example, language, different cultural beliefs and values, different cultural practices, and others.

   c Create a T-chart, listing *barriers* to positive cultural interactions. For each barrier, list a *solution*.

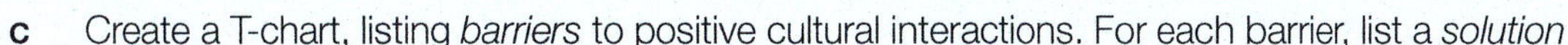

When two or more cultural groups interact, the culture and society of a country is impacted in the short and long term. There are many different types of relationships that can form between cultural groups. These relationships can remain the same or change over time due to a range of factors. The FOUR main types of relationships are described below. They are all **generalisations**.

- **Assimilation**. This is when a minority culture is completely absorbed by a more dominant culture. It might be a quick or a gradual change.
  Example: In the decades following the signing of the Treaty of Waitangi, the early New Zealand government attempted to assimilate Māori into British culture and way of life. The Hunn Report (1960) recommended that New Zealand move beyond 'assimilation' to 'integration'.
- **Integration**. This is when two different cultural groups accept one another and come together to create an entirely new culture over time. Importantly, both cultures remain distinct and alive.
  Example: The influx of Polynesian migrants to New Zealand since the mid-1970s has changed New Zealand's cultural identity with a Pacific Island influence.

- **Segregation**. This is when a particular cultural group is separated and isolated based on their race, class or ethnic origin in many or all aspects of daily life. This might include separate schools, housing areas and access to public facilities such as toilets, pools and parks. The opposite of segregation is **desegregation**.
  Example: Chinese gold miners came to New Zealand in the 1860s during the South Island gold rush and over the following decades faced widespread **racism** and prejudice from white New Zealanders. Newspapers at the time labelled this threat the 'Yellow Peril' and this racism led to a restriction on Chinese immigration and extra government taxes. In Dunedin, Chinese gold miners were banned from living in the town with Pākehā and couldn't be buried in local graveyards.
- **Exclusion**. This is when individuals and communities are discriminated against in society and are blocked from accessing basic rights. It may apply to a particular ethnic group, to people with disabilities, or to members of the LGBTI (Lesbian, Gay, Bisexual, Transgender and Intersex) community.
  Example: One modern-day example is the law that was passed in 2013 allowing same-sex couples to be married in New Zealand. Before 2013, same-sex couples were denied this right and discriminated against.

CHAPTER 3

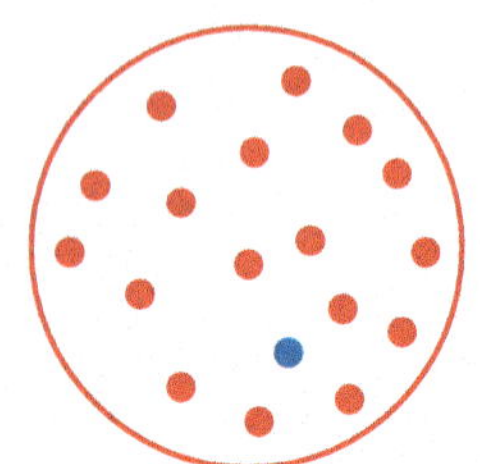

Assimilation

Blue people become red people

Integration

Red people and blue people are together.

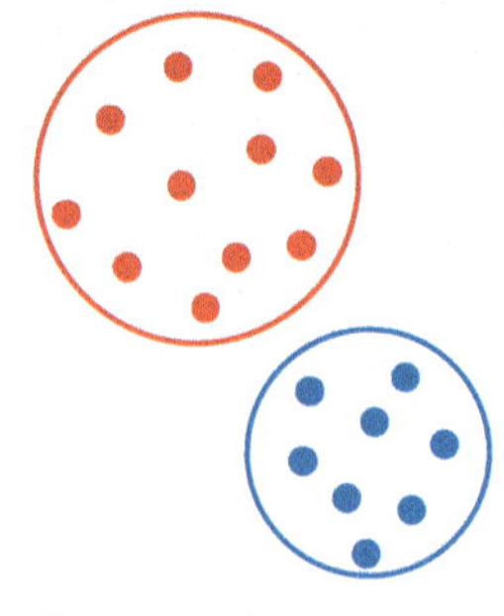

Segregation

Red people and blue people are separated.

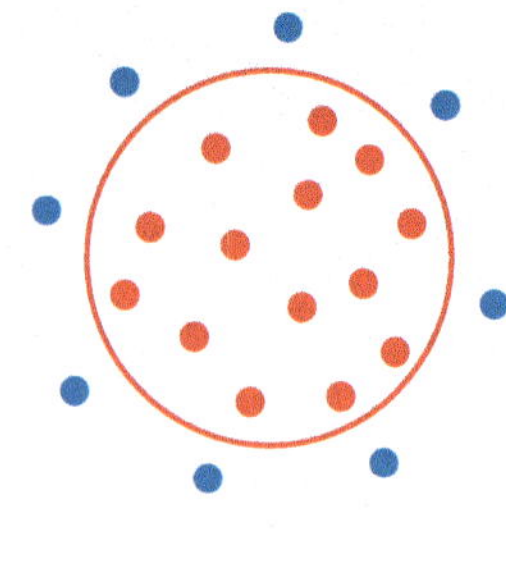

Exclusion

Red people keep blue people on the margins.

Activities

Independent

2 Each of the relationships above uses a complicated word to describe what is happening. Try to come up with at least three synonyms (a word with the same meaning) for each relationship which is easier for you to understand. One has been given for you to help you get started.

Assimilation	Integration
• Absorbed • ? • ? • ?	• Combined • ? • ? • ?
Segregation	**Exclusion**
• Kept apart • ? • ? • ?	• Left out • ? • ? • ?

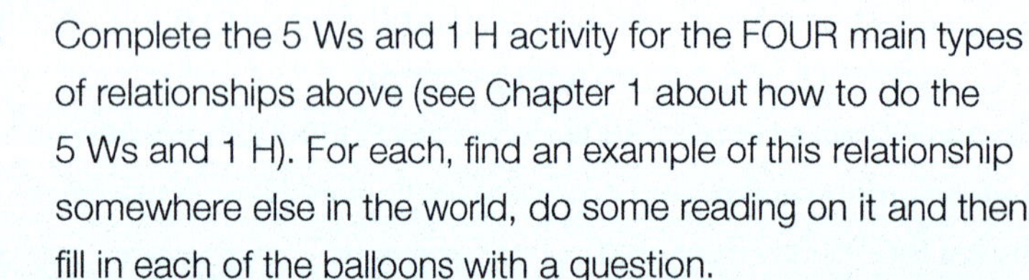

3 Complete the 5 Ws and 1 H activity for the FOUR main types of relationships above (see Chapter 1 about how to do the 5 Ws and 1 H). For each, find an example of this relationship somewhere else in the world, do some reading on it and then fill in each of the balloons with a question.

For example, for the cultural relationship of **Segregation**, you might choose the racial segregation of blacks and whites in the southern United States. Once you have filled in all of the balloons, answer your questions.

Cultural pluralism

Today New Zealand is a country with people from a diverse range of cultures. This is often called a multicultural society. However, there is also a new term that is now being used. The term is **cultural pluralism**. This term refers to all minority cultures within the larger society of New Zealand that still maintain their unique cultural identity. Furthermore, the values and practices of such minority cultures are supported and accepted by the wider culture.

ISBN: 9780170368117

First contact

Most of the early encounters between Māori and Europeans occurred without incident. However, there were several examples when violence did take place in the decades before the signing of the Treaty of Waitangi in 1840.

Activity

Independent

4 Violence and bloodshed in early New Zealand.

Four examples of this were:

- the burning of the *Boyd* in 1809
- the *Elizabeth* incident in 1830
- the *Harriet* affair in 1834
- war at Kororāreka (Russell) in 1845.

Build a 'brick wall' of 10 facts about one of these significant examples of violence and bloodshed in early New Zealand. Put one fact inside each brick. Write the name of your event above your brick wall.

The arrival of Europeans had a devastating effect on the Māori culture and way of life. A culture of people with different values, new religions, dangerous illnesses and new technologies had a **fatal impact** on the Māori. It was believed by some Europeans that the fatal impact and the effects of assimilation and **intermarriage** might eventually wipe out the Māori race in New Zealand.

Cause and effect

Cause = the reason for an event occurring.
Effect = what happened because of the event.
Cause + effect = explains why events happen the way they do.

Activity

Independent

5 Fill in the boxes below with three causes and three effects of the arrival of Europeans to New Zealand before 1840.

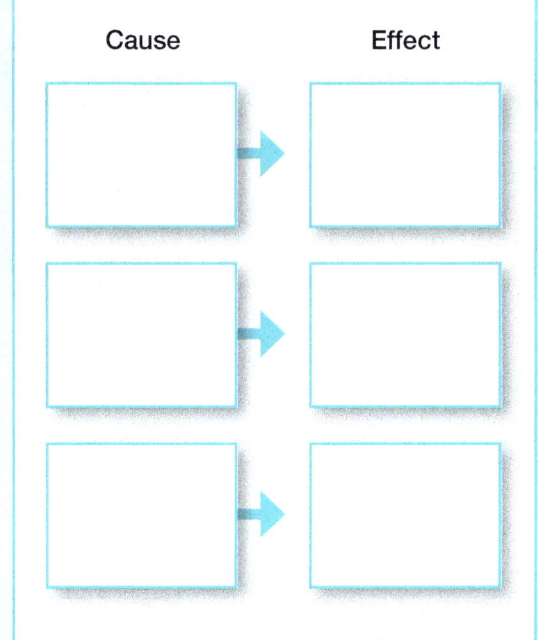

CHAPTER 3

DIVERSITY

Prejudice and discrimination

There are many things that influence a person's perspective and make them see things in a certain way. These include a person's upbringing, culture, gender, age and religion.

One of the biggest challenges faced by people who move to another country with a culture different from their own is how they will be able to live peacefully and happily and how they will adjust to another country's ways and still keep their own sense of cultural identity.

Many people still judge others by the colour of their skin. The underlying causes of **prejudice** (a feeling) and **discrimination** (an action) are similar around the world. A 2010 New Zealand Government report showed that the main reason people feel discriminated against and face prejudice in New Zealand is because of 'their skin colour, race, ethnicity or nationality'.

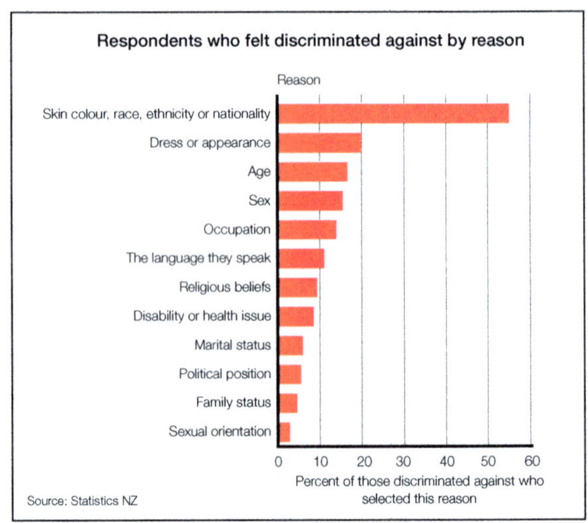

Activities

Independent

6 Below are THREE examples of cultural groups that have faced prejudice and discrimination in New Zealand's history. Choose ONE and research the following on the internet.

- 19th-century **Chinese** goldminers
- **Dalmatians** from Croatia in the 1890s
- **Germans** living in New Zealand during World War One and World War Two

a What was the time period during which the largest numbers of this group migrated to New Zealand?

b What was the **main** reason why they came to New Zealand?

c How were they treated differently? Why?

d What actions were taken to try to overcome the prejudice towards them?

e Have they resolved the issue or does this cultural group still face discrimination today?

 ISBN: 9780170368117

7 Use the internet to find *'Working together: Racial discrimination in New Zealand'* a short report on the Statistics New Zealand website.

a What is the source of this report?

b List all of the different reasons that have caused people to feel discriminated against.

c Have you felt discriminated against because of any of these reasons? If so, how many of these reasons?

d This report was released in 2010. Would the ranking of any of these reasons have changed since then? If you think so, which reason, and why?

Extra for experts

8 a How do individuals (past and present) influence the ways in which cultural interaction occurs?

b Using the definitions for **prejudice** and **discrimination**, identify how the attitudes and actions of individuals might influence cultural interaction.

Group

9 Who's *not* in our school?

a Consider which of the following groups are not at your school. For example:

- Girls or boys?
- Orphans?
- Refugees?
- Those with physical or mental disabilities?
- Those who have been in trouble with the law?

b Using the five groups above, answer the following questions.

- Which of these groups do not attend our school? Should they? Why, or why not?
- Do they attend a school elsewhere?
- Consider those who cannot physically attend a school. How can they receive an education?
- Do families have to pay for their children to attend our school? How much? Why?

Pair

10 a Why do some new immigrants feel it is difficult to meet and get to know their neighbours?

b In pairs, brainstorm what people in a neighbourhood could do to welcome new immigrants.

c What could new immigrant families do to welcome their new neighbours to their homes or activities?

Case study: The dawn raids

From the mid-1970s to the early 1980s, Polynesian immigrants were the targets of **dawn raids**. These operations involved special police squads raiding homes and workplaces, usually in the early hours of the morning, to seek out overstayers. Families would then be deported. One main reason for the dawn raids was that the New Zealand economy was in decline. The government at the time was looking for someone to blame. Polynesians became **scapegoats** for the New Zealand government to turn attention away from the economic problems it was facing at the time.

CHAPTER 3

The response to the injustice and unfair treatment towards the Polynesians, especially Samoans and Tongans, led to new groups being formed. One group was called the **Polynesian Panthers**. They had been influenced by the American Black Panthers, who were fighting for black civil rights in the United States. The Polynesian Panthers challenged the use of **derogatory** terms such as 'overstayer', 'fresh off the boat' and 'coconut'.

Even today, cultural groups in New Zealand are still facing discrimination. The war in the Middle East against the terrorist group ISIS (the Islamic State), which began in 2014, has renewed prejudice and increased discrimination towards Muslim New Zealanders.

Activities

Pair

11 OPV – Other Points of View.

Complete the following based on your understanding of the dawn raids. You might need to do some more research and reading about who was involved and what happened.

- **a** Identify all of the people and groups affected by the dawn raids.
- **b** Identify the views of each individual/group affected.

Independent

12 What are some other examples in New Zealand of when a specific ethnic or cultural group has become the scapegoat for a problem or issue?

Refugees

Activity

Independent

13 What do you already know?

Copy the chart below. Fill in the first two columns of the KWL (Know, Want, Learned) chart based on the topic: Refugees. Then continue with Chapter 3. Come back to this chart and fill in the final column with what you have learned about refugees.

What do you already (K)NOW?	What do you (W)ANT to know?	What have you (L)EARNED?

 ISBN: 9780170368117

Ever since there has been war, discrimination and intolerance, there have been refugees. Since the end of World War Two in 1945, New Zealand has taken more than 20,000 refugees. New Zealand is one of just a few countries that has an official refugee quota. In 2018, New Zealand's annual refugee quota went up for the first time since 1987 – from 750 per year to 1000. However, many people think we should be taking more. The global demand for the resettlement of refugees is high.

Refugee camp, Democratic Republic of Congo, 2008.

In 2015, the world's first climate change refugee arrived in New Zealand from Kiribati. Kiribati is one of the lowest-lying nations on Earth. Ioane Teitiota claimed that he was fleeing the rising sea levels in his Pacific Island homeland.

Activities

Independent

14 Carry out an inquiry on refugees who have come to New Zealand to help you complete the following questions.

- **a** What is a refugee?
- **b** Name FIVE different countries that New Zealand has accepted refugees from?
- **c** Why does New Zealand allow refugees to live here?
- **d** What criteria should be used in selecting who can come and live here permanently?
- **e** What is the name of the organisation that runs the resettlement programme for refugees in New Zealand? What does the resettlement programme involve?
- **f** What might be some of the problems that refugees face when settling into life in New Zealand?

Class

15 Creating a human continuum.

A continuum is a continuous line between two extremes to show how people feel about a particular issue. One extreme, represented by one side of your classroom, will be completely AGAINST the following statement. The other extreme, represented by the other side of your classroom, will be completely FOR the following statement. If you stand in the middle of the continuum you are neither for nor against the statement, that is, you are neutral. Your teacher will tell you which end of the classroom is FOR and which AGAINST for your human continuum.

100% FOR	NEUTRAL neither for nor against	100% AGAINST

Decide what your personal opinion is on the following statement:
New Zealand, with all of our open spaces and resources, should allow all refugees who wish to settle here.

Once you have decided what you feel about this particular statement, stand up and place yourself on this imaginary human continuum in your classroom.

ISBN: 9780170368117

- **a** Have a look at those around you. Where are most of you standing?
- **b** What does this tell you about the statement?
- **c** If this activity were done using everyone in New Zealand, would the continuum be different to the one that your class has created? Why/why not?
- **d** What could be done to change people's opinions about this particular issue?

Independent

16 Go to the United Nations Refugee Agency (UNHCR) website. Find the gallery that lists 200 prominent refugees who have made a difference. Refugees such as Albert Einstein are included. Choose one refugee from the list. Read their profile and summarise the information provided. Make sure to include key points of information such as their name, profession, country of origin, country of asylum, date of birth/death and any interesting facts.

17 On the run!

Pretend that you have to flee from your homeland. You have five minutes to pack. Make a list of five items that you would quickly pack to take with you. Next to each item, write a reason for why you chose this item.

Group

18 Discussing a controversial issue.

Issue: Should doctors from overseas be allowed to practise in New Zealand?

Consider the issue and discuss with those in your group. Complete the following using a copy of the chart below.

- **a** In a T-chart make a list of the points **FOR** and **AGAINST** doctors from overseas being given employment in New Zealand.
- **b** Make a list of the **alternatives** that could help to resolve the problem.
- **c** Make a list of all of the possible **consequences** that could happen if doctors from overseas are employed.
- **d** Make a list of all of the possible **consequences** that could happen if they are not given the opportunity to practise.
- **e** What might be the preferred **solution** to resolve this issue?
- **f** What might be a form of **social action** that you could take to support these doctors?

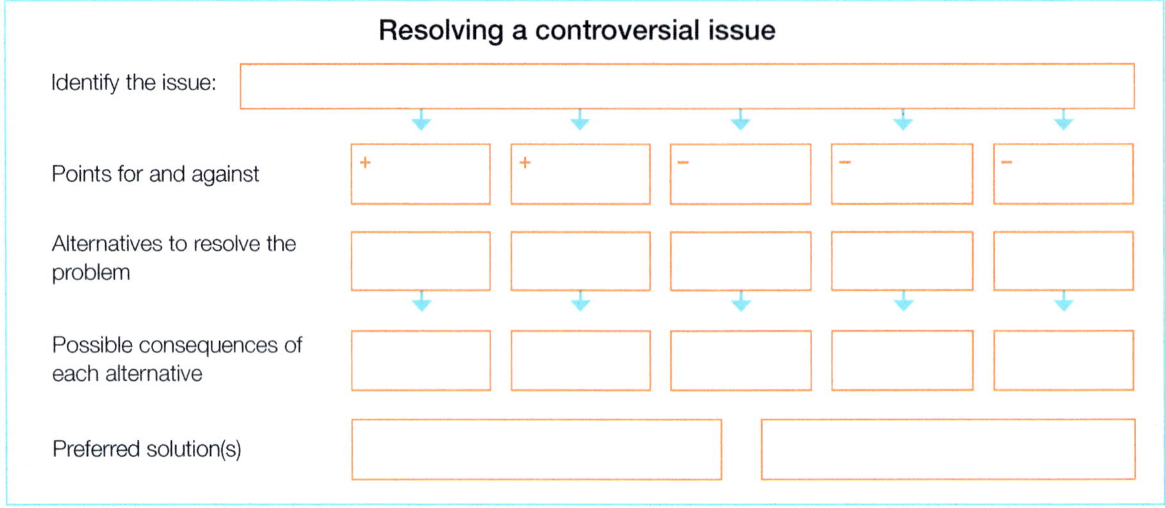

ISBN: 9780170368117

Working to find solutions: no place for hate

Today, there are a number of official and government organisations in New Zealand that support individuals and groups in need and give people a place to take their complaints of unfair treatment. Some examples of such groups include the Waitangi Tribunal, the Human Rights Commission and the Race Relations Office.

The following are some ways you can create a prejudice-free zone in your home, school and community.

- Be mindful of your language; avoid stereotypical remarks and challenge those made by others.
- Invite a guest speaker who is a recognised civil or human rights leader in your community to address your school assembly.
- Form a student committee to write 'Rules of Respect' for your school and display the finished set of rules in every classroom.
- Become aware of the demographics of your local community and compare it to towns and cities to better understand the cultural diversity in your community.
- Meet with school and community librarians and local bookstores to discuss ways to include more literature that is representative of all of the cultures in your community.

Activities

Independent

19 What are some other ways you can create a prejudice-free zone that you could add to this list?

Class

20 Practise responding to racist remarks.

Speaking out against acts of discrimination can be difficult. Working in small groups, talk about an act of discrimination that you have heard about or personally experienced. It could be someone making a stereotypical remark, a put-down or someone telling a racist joke.

In groups, brainstorm how those involved could have responded positively to the racism. Re-enact the scene but this time incorporate some ideas from the rest of the class to have a more positive outcome.

Once you have finished, then watch the other groups perform their re-enactment and contribute your own suggestions.

Independent

21 Find a newspaper article online about when someone has been the target of racial abuse recently in New Zealand. Write at least ONE paragraph in which you summarise the article that you have found and read.

22 Write a statement on what you have learned about racism.

23 Create a poster or write a poem promoting cultural tolerance and understanding.

The Universal Declaration of Human Rights

The United Nations is a world organisation that aims to maintain peace and security. The Universal Declaration of Human Rights (UDHR) is a document adopted by the United Nations General Assembly in 1948 after World War Two. It was the first time that a group of people had written down a list of rights that applied to everyone in the world. The declaration has 30 articles (or parts). The full text is published on the United Nations website. The following articles are relevant:

- (Right to equality) UDHR Article 1: You are born free and equal in rights to every other human being. You have the ability to think and to tell right from wrong. You should treat others with friendship.
- (Right to nationality and the freedom to change it) UDHR Article 15: (1) You have the right to belong to a country and have a nationality. (2) No one can take away your nationality without a good reason.
- (Right to participate in the cultural life of your community) UDHR Article 27: (1) You have the right to participate in the traditions and learning of your community, to enjoy the arts and to benefit from scientific progress.

In 2001, UNESCO adopted the Universal Declaration on Cultural Diversity. It proclaimed that human rights included the rights of different cultures. UNESCO recognised for the first time that cultural diversity is a common part of humanity and must be preserved and protected.

An interview with Dame Susan Devoy

Dame Susan Devoy has been New Zealand's Race Relations Commissioner working for the Human Rights Commission since 2013. The following are her responses in an interview for *Diversity* in November 2015.

Read the following extracts from the interview and then answer the questions that follow.

What is your cultural background?

I am a Pākehā New Zealander of Irish descent. My father immigrated to New Zealand with his parents in 1923.

Why is it important for people to understand their cultural identity?

Everyone needs to have a sense of belonging and part of that is an understanding of where you come from and your place in the world.

What is so cool about Aotearoa New Zealand?

Aotearoa New Zealand is one of the most ethnically diverse countries on this planet, in fact Auckland is now considered super diverse with over 40% of the population having been born overseas. This change in demographic has given rise to a multicultural society and has provided many different opportunities and experiences for all Kiwis to enjoy.

Is there racism in New Zealand?

Yes, sadly we know that **discrimination exists in our society especially for those who are *visually diverse***. We all need to take responsibility for this and stand up for each other. Racism is another form of bullying and we need to know that the victims of racial abuse are not alone by calling it when we see it.

 ISBN: 9780170368117

What ways can we show our acceptance of other cultures?

We need to make the effort to walk a mile in someone else's shoes. Often prejudice is born from a lack of understanding and intolerance. We all need to understand that welcoming a migrant to our country means enabling them to live and understand the Kiwi way of life but to accept that maintaining their own culture is both accepted and welcome.

Why is immigration to New Zealand such an issue for people?

Change for many people is difficult to accept; the face of New Zealand has changed. One in ten New Zealanders are Asian Kiwis; in Auckland it is one in four. We need to fully appreciate that there has, and always be, immigration and as a small country we need this to grow both economically and socially. There are many issues facing all New Zealanders and we need to discuss these reasonably and rationally without placing the blame on entire ethnic groups.

How many refugees should New Zealand take each year?

I believe we have the capacity to double our annual quota from 750 to 1500. This is well overdue.

Is cultural diversity a good thing?

Of course but we need to plan for our future. We have a very good record of race relations in New Zealand but we can and should do better. New Zealand is also one of the most peaceful countries on earth and to maintain and enhance that reputation we must all take responsibility for how we treat others. Human rights begin at home, in our schools, our work places, our communities. The legacy we leave behind for our children and grandchildren is up to us!

CHAPTER 3

Activity

Independent

24 Complete the following questions:

- **a** Find out more about Dame Susan Devoy. Make a list of some of her previous achievements before she became the Race Relations Commissioner in 2013.
- **b** When was the Human Rights Commission set up, and what piece of legislation does it work under?
- **c** Name three other commissioners of the Human Rights Commission and say what their roles are.
- **d** What are some of the important qualities or characteristics that the Race Relations Commissioner would have to possess?
- **e** Devoy says that '…**discrimination exists in our society especially for those who are *visually diverse***.' What might the phrase 'visually diverse' mean?
- **f** Devoy also says that '**We need to make the effort to walk a mile in someone else's shoes.**' Brainstorm at least three different ways that you could try to experience what it would be like to live as another culture lives.
- **g** What response from Devoy do you find most interesting and why?
- **h** If you were interviewing Devoy, what would be TWO questions that you would like to ask her?

Stereotypes: beat 'em or join 'em

Stereotypes are learned beliefs. We learn them from our parents, peers and the media. It is a way that we simplify the world around us and try to understand the society in which we live. Stereotypes are usually formed for a specific group of people. The major disadvantage with stereotypes is that it makes us ignore rerekētanga (differences) between individuals. It also causes us to think things about people that are probably not true. Most stereotypes are negative.

Cultural cruise control is when young people think that their beliefs and cultural values are the same as everyone else's. It leads to stereotypes because they are not aware of how the other person thinks and they make judgements of them. Developing **cultural intelligence** (**CQ**) leads to a better awareness of others and will help to overcome assumptions.

DIVERSITY

Activities

Group

25 **a** Below are three negative racial stereotypes. Discuss them in your group and answer the following for each: Where has this stereotype come from? Why does it still continue today?

- i Asians are bad drivers.
- ii Black male teenagers are good athletes.
- iii All Muslims are terrorists.

b Make a list of all of the other racial stereotypes you have read or heard people say.

Class

26 Discuss the following.

- **a** How do people learn to make stereotypes? How might they unlearn them?
- **b** Can you think of any events in world history that were influenced by stereotypes and biases?
- **c** How can the media (internet, TV, movies) help to reduce stereotyping?

ISBN: 9780170368117

d Do you think certain ethnic or cultural groups are more targeted for stereotyping than others? If so, why?

e What do you think an individual can do to help reduce racism and overcome stereotyping?

Extra for experts

27 a Define the term 'cultural glass ceiling'.

b Does a 'cultural glass ceiling' exist in New Zealand workplaces for people of different culture? Explain.

Time to recap

1 What is the most significant thing you have learned in this chapter? Why?

2 'The Muddiest Point'. Write down which part of this chapter was difficult to understand. Compare what you wrote down with someone else. Find someone in the class who can explain it to you.

CHAPTER 3

ISBN: 9780170368117

4

EXPRESS YOURSELF!

'It's not the mountain we conquer, but ourselves.'

— Sir Edmund Hillary, New Zealand mountaineer and explorer

Learning intentions

After studying this chapter you should understand that:

- cultural practices vary but reflect similar purposes
- people pass on and sustain culture and heritage for different reasons and that this has consequences for people.

Useful words

traditional — following an established set of beliefs or customs.

diversify — to give variety.

foodie — a person with specific interest in food.

New Zealand has many thriving cultural communities with a wide range of cultural and heritage practices. Migrants and refugees have contributed to New Zealand in many ways. This chapter will look at the following aspects, which celebrate the individual, group and cultural diversity of Aotearoa New Zealand:

- **Traditional arts**
- **Festivals**
- **Food**
- **Religion**
- **Education**.

DIVERSITY

Traditional arts

Arts are an expression of identity and an example of a living heritage. Knowledge is passed down from one generation to the next. Māori visual arts are spiritual, highly stylised and provide information about whakapapa. Styles of art form vary from region to region across New Zealand. There are three main Māori traditional art forms:

- **Carving**
- **Weaving**
- **Tā moko (tattooing)**.

Carving

Carving, or whakairo, is an art form that has been done by Māori for many centuries. The three most commonly used materials are greenstone (pounamu), wood and bone. Māori carving is among the best in the world.

 ISBN: 9780170368117

Activity

Independent

1 Copy and fill in this table using information from the internet.

Material	What is this material used to make? (Give at least three examples.)	Name two famous New Zealand carvers.	Name a public space or museum where a piece is on display.
Greenstone (pounamu)			
Wood			
Bone			

Weaving

Weaving is traditionally an art form done by Māori women. *Piupiu* (short skirts) for men and women are made from strands of curled dried flax (harakeke). Harakeke is also used to make *kete* (bags), headbands and mats. *Korowai* (cloaks) are weaved together from dog's skin or feathers and are used at special ceremonies. *Tukutuku* are woven reed panels displayed in wharenui (meeting houses). *Poi* are also made and are used in poi dances.

The art of weaving was in serious decline until the 1950s when moves were made to preserve and promote the traditional Māori art. The Māori Weavers of New Zealand (Te Roopu Raranga Whatu o Aotearoa) was established in 1983 by the Māori and South Pacific Arts Council. Since the early 2000s, weaving has returned as a traditional visual art form for modern Māori expression.

CHAPTER 4

Activity

Independent

2 There are five words italicised above. For each, find an image and write at least ONE paragraph describing how each item is traditionally made, what materials are used in the weaving process, and, if dyes are used, how and why?

Tā moko (tattooing)

Tattooing is seen throughout the Pacific. Moko are proud symbols of Māori culture and are a gateway into one's past. Moko were traditionally applied with sharpened bone needles to cut deeply into the skin, bone chisels and a dye made from charcoal mixed with plant oil. Even with modern tattooing instruments, the process is painful. Men might have moko on their whole face. A woman's moko is generally applied on the lips and chin. There has been a significant resurgence in tattooing (today popularly known as 'inking') since the early 2000s as a sign of cultural and tribal identity, and a sense of belonging.

ISBN: 9780170368117

Activities

Independent

3 Carry out further reading on tā moko. You might have a book in the library or you might be able to use the internet. Complete the following questions based on your understanding of tā moko.
   a What is tā moko?
   b Describe the Māori myth of how the art form of tā moko came to New Zealand.
   c Describe the traditional process for getting a moko.
   d What technology is used today for getting a moko?
   e It is considered culturally inappropriate for non-Māori to get a moko. Why is this?
   f Find the names of three famous celebrities who have got a traditional Māori tattoo in New Zealand.

Pair

4 Three-circle Venn diagram.

A Venn diagram is made up of overlapping circles. It allows you to identify similarities and differences. Use this graphic organiser to describe similarities and differences between the three main traditional art forms of carving, weaving and tā moko.

Where the circles overlap, write shared characteristics (things that are the same). In the circles to the left, right and bottom, list the features that are specific (things that are different) to each of the traditional Māori art forms.

Three-circle Venn diagram

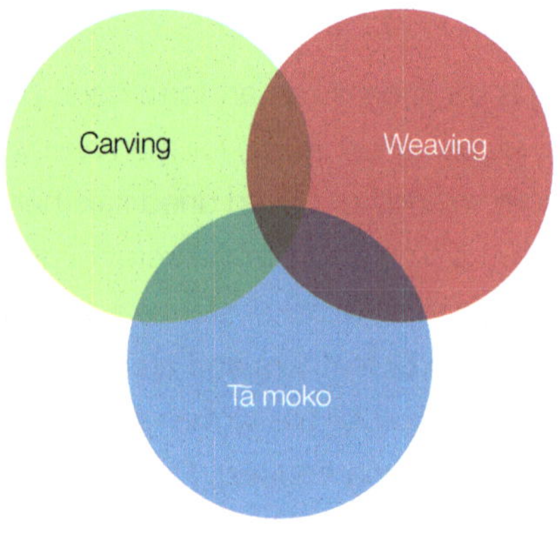

DIVERSITY

The *pe'a* in New Zealand

Māori are not the only cultural group in New Zealand that tattoo. When many Polynesians migrated to New Zealand in the 1960s and 1970s, they brought with them these practices. Today, Pacific Island tattooing is strongest among the Samoan community. The *pe'a* is the name for the traditional male tattoo for Samoans. The *pe'a* covers the body from the waist to the knees and the process, carried out by a *tufuga ta tatau* (master tattooist), is very painful. It takes many weeks to complete and is considered a rite of passage for Samoan boys into manhood. The *pe'a* symbolises bravery, leadership, maturity and honour to one's family and culture.

Samoan women also get tattooed. A woman's *pe'a* tattoo (known as a *malu*) is tattooed from below the knee to the top of the thigh. Sometimes the *malu* is done on the hands or lower abdomen.

In 2013, following a backlash from members of the Samoan community, Nike pulled its new tattoo sports clothing design for women off the shelves in New Zealand. It proved to be too controversial, as the women's leggings gave the appearance of a *pe'a* — a cultural and deeply symbolic tattoo reserved for men.

ISBN: 9780170368117

Activities

Independent

5 Choose two of the following Pacific Island cultures in New Zealand that has a practice of tattooing: Cook Islands, Fijian, Tongan, Tahitian.

Complete the following questions for each of the two cultural groups.

a What is the word for the male tattoo and for the female tattoo?

b At what age do people traditionally get tattooed?

c What part of the male and female body gets tattooed?

d What is *similar* about the style of tattoos with other Pacific Island cultures?

e What is *different* about the style of tattoos with other Pacific Island cultures?

Pair

6 Many schools in New Zealand now have rules around students having visible cultural tattoos. Find out if your school has rules on whether cultural tattoos can be visible or need to be hidden. If so, how do they manage and enforce this rule?

Other coming-of-age ceremonies in New Zealand

Coming of age is a young person's transition from being a child to being an adult. There are many cultural and religious ceremonies that take place in New Zealand every year. We have already looked at the *pe'a*, the Samoan tattoo, which marks the journey into manhood for Samoan boys. Below are some other coming-of-age ceremonies.

- Getting a *nifo koula*, or gold tooth, for Tongans.
- Niuean boys getting their hair cut.
- The Indian Hindu ceremony of *Ritu Kala*, when a girl wears a sari for the first time.
- The New Zealand 21st birthday party celebration.

CHAPTER 4

Activity

Independent

7 Choose one of the coming-of-age ceremonies, or find your own one, and write a two-paragraph description of the ceremony. The first paragraph should *describe the history of the ceremony* and the second paragraph should *describe how the ceremony takes place today*.

ISBN: 9780170368117

Many New Zealand sports teams now use cultural heritage jerseys with Māori and Pasifika designs for certain games. These teams include Super Rugby, NZ Māori and the Warriors.

Activity

Independent

8 What do you already know?

Copy this chart. Fill in the first two columns of the KWL (Know, Want, Learned) chart based on the topic: Cultural and local festivals in New Zealand. Then continue with this first part of the chapter. Come back to this chart and fill in the final column with what you have learned about cultural and local festivals in New Zealand.

What do you already (K)NOW?	What do you (W)ANT to know?	What have you (L)EARNED?

DIVERSITY

Festivals

Why do we have festivals?

One of the most visible ways that we get to experience another culture is through festivals and celebrations. This is by being a part of the social activities, food, rituals and exhibitions of the festival. Festivals play a very important role in New Zealand as expressions of heritage, culture and tradition. They are living cultural treasures. They become something to look forward to each year and are a way to pass knowledge and traditions on to the next generation and retain an important sense of identity. Festivals show the acceptance of cultural diversity. They also add a creative buzz, colour, fun and a special atmosphere to the city in which they are hosted. Cultural festivals can include performing arts (music, dance and song) and oral traditions.

Matariki: Māori New Year

Matariki is a small cluster of stars, also known as the Pleiades. For Māori, the most important time of the year is **Matariki**, the Māori New Year. Traditionally, Māori have recognised the rise of Matariki as a time to remember those who have passed away and to prepare for the New Year celebrations. With the food stores full, a hangi is held and attended by visitors. Kites help to mark the occasion. By the time Matariki comes into the sky, you must have finished the preserving of kai and it is the right time for planting. The never-ending cycle of seasons is marked out in Aotearoa by the movement of the stars. No one anywhere else in the world sees the sky as we do.

Manu Aute Kite Day

As a part of the annual Matariki celebrations, kite days are held across the country. In Auckland, at Ōrākei marae, kites are flown. Māori believe that kites connect the heavens to the earth.

 ISBN: 9780170368117

ASB Polyfest

ASB Polyfest celebrated its 40th year in 2015. It is the world's biggest Māori and Pacific Island cultural festival and continues to grow bigger every year. In 2016, the Diversity Stage featured Chinese, Indian, Filipino and Malaysian performers among over 50 other ethnic groups from all cultures, joining together and learning from one another.

Chinese New Year: the Lantern Festival

A major holiday in many Asian cultures, the Chinese New Year is a very important Chinese festival that has been celebrated for over 2000 years. However, the Chinese New Year doesn't fall on 1 January like it does in New Zealand. Chinese New Year begins sometime between mid-January and mid-February and ends with the Lantern Festival 14 days later. In New Zealand, the Lantern Festival has been celebrated publicly since the year 2000, and has become increasingly popular in a number of cities. Chinese are the largest non-European, non-Pacific Island cultural group in New Zealand, so the Chinese New Year celebration is becoming a more and more culturally significant festival every year.

Activity

Independent

9 Find out which of the 12 animals of the Chinese zodiac you are. Does the animal match your personality?

Eid: The end of Ramadan

Eid is a religious holiday observed worldwide by Muslims. It marks the end of the 30-day fast through the Islamic holy month of Ramadan. Celebrated in Auckland since 2011, Auckland Eid Day is a biannual event that celebrates the two annual Islamic holidays of Eid al-Adha and Eid al-Fitr. Eid aims to bring together all Muslim ethnicities in an atmosphere of fun, happiness and unity. Traditional prayer is followed by games, food and a variety of stage and cultural performances.

ISBN: 9780170368117

Diwali: the Festival of Lights

Celebrated in New Zealand since 2002, Diwali is an ancient and significant five-day festival in Indian culture. It celebrates the triumph of light over darkness and the renewal of life. Festivals are held in Auckland and Wellington at some point between mid-October and mid-November each year and it is a chance to enjoy traditional and modern Indian culture. During Diwali, people clean their homes and light lamps and candles inside and outside. A popular thing that people do at Diwali is get their hands decorated with henna designs.

WOMAD

WOMAD (World of Music, Arts and Dance) is an international arts festival that takes place annually at the Bowl of Brooklands in New Plymouth. WOMAD consists of a very large and varying range of cultural and indigenous musicians and groups from around the world. Through embracing music, WOMAD allows audiences to gain an insight into other cultures.

Activities

Independent

10 Write a statement on what you have learned about cultural festivals in New Zealand.

11 What cultural festivals do you know of that are held in your town or city? Find the name of one and complete the following.

- a Does the festival originate from a specific culture, religion or other group?
- b What time of year is it held? Why?
- c How often is it held?
- d Where is it held?
- e What activities take place?
- f Does it celebrate a special occasion? If so, explain.
- g How could the festival be of interest to other cultural groups?

 ISBN: 9780170368117

Pair

12 What do council and community groups do to attract people to festivals in your town or city? Brainstorm as many ideas as you can think of. For example, free to attend, family friendly, and so on.

13 Create a 'cultural kete'.

Brainstorm and write down 10 artefacts that you would include in your 'cultural kete' to give to someone from another country. Each artefact must represent a different cultural group in New Zealand.

For example, to represent Māori culture you might want to put a piece of carved pounamu in your 'cultural kete'.

Draw your 10 artefacts or get images of them from the internet. For each artefact, write two or three sentences explaining what it is and why you have included it.

Local festivals

Cultural festivals don't have to involve just specific cultural groups. Many local towns and regions across New Zealand have their own unique annual celebrations. Some of these include:

- Wings over Wairarapa
- Naseby Ice Festival
- Kawhia Kai Festival
- Hokitika Wildfoods Festival
- Bluff Oyster and Food Festival
- Waiheke Olive Festival
- The Great NZ Muster
- Ragamuffin
- Golden Shears
- Southland Festival of the Arts
- Auckland Anniversary Day Regatta
- Art Deco Weekend in Napier
- Thames Heritage Week
- Bay of Islands Country Rock Festival

Activity

Independent

14 What other local festivals do you know of?

Food

Traditional Māori kai (food) included key ingredients such as kūmara (sweet potato), taro, yam, birds and fish. Kai was cooked in earth ovens, known as *hāngi*.

After the arrival of British settlers, Māori began to adapt many of their foods and ingredients. In the 19th century (1801 CE – 1900 CE), the dominant food culture became British as settlers tried as much as possible to cook and prepare the same foods from their homeland. This became known as the 'meat and three veg' tradition.

ISBN: 9780170368117

A *hāngi* is a traditional method of cooking that is found throughout the Pacific. A pit is dug one metre deep. Layers of wood are put in it with stones placed on top and it is set alight. When the stones are hot enough, wet leaves or sacks are put over them. Pork, chicken, beef, kūmara and other vegetables are placed on top in woven flax baskets. These days, the baskets are often made of wire and the food wrapped in tin foil. More wet leaves/sacks are put on top and soil is shovelled on top. It takes more than three hours to cook the food. It is then dug up and served hot.

These images are from the Waiheke High School Matariki hāngi celebrated every year. Many hours of preparation are put in by the whole school and wider community to prepare the food for the Matariki celebrations.

DIVERSITY

Activity

Group

15 Discussion.

Practise *listening* to the other person talk and then take your turn to *articulate* what you think. Why did the early British settlers to New Zealand want to prepare and eat food that was familiar to them?

It wasn't until the late 1950s, as cultural diversity began to increase in New Zealand, that our cuisine began to **diversify**. New Zealanders began to embrace food from other cultures, especially from Mediterranean and Asian countries. By 1960, most major cities in New Zealand could proudly boast one Chinese restaurant.

However, in the past 30 years this has changed significantly.

 ISBN: 9780170368117

In recent decades, fast food and dining out have taken centre stage, with a diverse range of ethnic cuisine now available. Ethnic restaurants also play an important role as cultural meeting places. Places like the Ōtara markets in South Auckland have a wide range of Pasifika foods available. Speciality stores have been established catering to specific ethnic tastes such as South African shops and Asian supermarkets. Cultural diversity linked with culinary innovation has established New Zealand today as a world destination for '**foodies**'.

One food that has not disappeared even with such fast-changing cultural diversity is the meat pie. The meat pie is seen throughout New Zealand and even though you can now order a butter chicken pie or a bok choy and carrot pie, the humble mince and cheese and steak pies remain. (Lamingtons and scones are two other examples of foods that have remained in New Zealand — yum!)

Activities

CHAPTER 4

Pair

16 Yummy foods from around the world!

Make a list of all of the different meals that you can now buy and enjoy in New Zealand. Some examples have been given for you: paella, samosa, ratatouille, ...

Independent

17 Food.

- a Write down everything you have eaten in the last two days.
- b Put a tick next to the food that is not traditional for people from your culture.
- c Look at the number of ticks you have, and write a sentence about how much your choice of food has been affected by cultural diversity in Aotearoa New Zealand.

ISBN: 9780170368117

Religion

Religious diversity is an important part of cultural diversity. Increasing cultural diversity has changed New Zealand from a country where the only places of worship were Christian churches to a country that now also has temples, mosques and synagogues as places of worship. This has led New Zealanders to recognise that there are many different religions in the world, which can exist quite peacefully alongside each other if people are prepared to treat one another with respect.

In 2004, 95 Jewish graves were vandalised in a cemetery in Wellington. Public outrage led the Human Rights Commission and community groups to establish the **Diversity Action Programme: Te Ngira** in New Zealand. The members of this group work to promote better relationships between diverse cultural groups and recognise equality. There is an annual forum, called the **New Zealand Diversity Forum**, which teaches positive race relations and good practice on cultural diversity. It is illegal in New Zealand to discriminate based on religious beliefs, and a number of different interfaith organisations support and protect this right.

Activity

Independent

18 Find out what is White Sunday.

The Human Rights Act 1993

The New Zealand Human Rights Act 1993 states that everyone has the right to:

- freedom of religion and belief
- express their belief, and
- follow the practices that arise from that belief.

The Diversity Fern

The logo of the New Zealand Diversity Action Programme represents the growing cultural diversity of New Zealand.

Baby fronds symbolising new growth

Middle Eastern (Iranian motif)

Vietnamese motif

Indian paisley motif

Traditional Chinese character

Samoan tapa cloth pattern

European Fleur de Lys (St Patrick's Cathedral, Auckland)

Māori kōwhaiwhai pattern (Manutuke Church)

The Diversity Fern was designed by Jean Voon.

www.hrc.co.nz/diversity 0800 496 877 infoline@hrc.co.nz

Human Rights Commission

ISBN: 9780170368117

Having a census in New Zealand

A census has been conducted in New Zealand ever since 1851. A census gathers information about a country, including population, people's age, jobs, income and where people live. It is how we get an up-to-date idea of what's really happening in New Zealand. This is because everyone is counted, including babies and visitors from overseas. It allows for long-term changes to be measured. Statistics New Zealand puts together all of the data and publishes the results in tables and reports online. These are free to access online.

Activities

Independent

19 Complete the following questions.

- **a** How often is a census held in New Zealand?
- **b** The 2013 census in New Zealand was set to be held in 2011, as the previous census was in 2006. Why was the 2011 census cancelled?
- **c** Where have you seen statistics being used in everyday life?

20 Go to www.stats.govt.nz and search 'ethnicity'. Carry out some data collection for the last three censuses from the tables of information provided for the following categories:

- Ethnic groups in New Zealand
- Birthplace and people born overseas
- Languages spoken
- Religious affiliation.

Once you have collected enough data, write a number of concluding sentences using the data. For example:

The first category is on 'Ethnic groups in New Zealand'. One Asian ethnic group that is listed is Filipino. The data provided for the numbers of people who identified as Filipino in the last three censuses were:

- 2001: 11,091 people
- 2006: 16,938 people
- 2013: 40,350 people.

Using this data, we can conclude that the Filipino population has more than tripled since 2001, from 11,091 people in 2001 to 40,350 people in 2013.

21 Complete the following questions and tasks based on the 2013 New Zealand census.

- **a** Rank the top five Christian religions (by numbers of followers) in 2013. Graph your results. Choose a graph that would be appropriate. (See Skill 3: Understanding Graphs, page 5.)
- **b** What number of people were members of the Sikh religion in 2006? In 2013?
- **c** What number of people were members of the Hindu religion in 2006? In 2013?
- **d** What number of people were members of the Muslim religion in 2006? In 2013?
- **e** What number of people in 2013 reported having no religion? Has this increased or decreased since 2006?

Education

Having a wide range of different cultures in a society causes change and creates opportunities for learning. Having teenagers from diverse backgrounds in our classes at school has increased the cultural awareness of many New Zealand students. It has also made teachers more aware of the needs and preferences of individuals, and this has benefited all students. Many students who come to New Zealand from other countries find that the attitudes and rules are very different here. Teachers from many different countries have come to work in New Zealand, and these teachers share their own cultural values and experiences. However, the richness of cultures in Auckland schools is very different to some parts of New Zealand. For example, if you were to go into a classroom in Otago or Southland, the students might still mostly be European.

The biggest issue in schools by far is language. ELL (English Language Learners) and ESOL (English for Speakers of Other Languages) departments are now common at most schools in New Zealand.

A programme called Confucius Classrooms has been set up in Auckland to cater for Chinese language and teaching. By 2016, eight schools across Auckland have signed up. Confuscious Classrooms (CCs) are school-based hubs for Chinese teaching and learning. In 2016 there are 12 CC schools, all based in Auckland.

The numbers

English for Speakers of Other Languages (ESOL) in New Zealand

34,000 students

1342 schools

157 ethnic groups

166 countries

126 different languages

1 school in Auckland has 345 ESOL kids ... but some schools in Otago and Southland have only one

DIVERSITY

 ISBN: 9780170368117

Activities

Independent

22 Complete the following questions.

- **a** In your classes, what different cultural perspectives are taught?
- **b** Why is it important to learn about the perspectives of other cultures?
- **c** What specific cultural groups are recognised within your school? One example could be having a Māori performing arts cultural group at your school.

Group

23 Imagine that a new student is joining your class. They have come from a different country. You need to plan a special welcome.

In groups, brainstorm different ideas for how you could welcome them to your school and to New Zealand.

Extra for experts

24 **a** Suggest some reasons why many students who come to New Zealand from other countries value study and achieve highly.

b What is the role of schools in assisting new migrants attending the school?

Time to recap

1 What is the most significant thing you have learned in this chapter? Why?

2 'The Muddiest Point'. Write down which part of this chapter was difficult to understand. Compare what you wrote down with someone else. Find someone in the class who can explain it to you.

CHAPTER 4

ISBN: 9780170368117

5

MAKING AOTEAROA COOL

'Represent this Nesian style all day, every night ...'

— from the song 'Nesian Style' by Nesian Mystik

Learning intentions

After studying this chapter you should understand that:

- cultural practices vary but reflect similar purposes
- people pass on and sustain culture and heritage for different reasons and that this has consequences for people.

Useful words

medium — the means by which something is communicated or expressed.

mandate — an official order to do something.

genre — a style of music, literature or art.

contemporary — present-day.

marginalise — to make a person or group seem unimportant.

Today, Aotearoa New Zealand has one of the most vibrant, diverse and experimental performing arts and cultural scenes in the world. These forms of expression allow people and groups from a range of cultures to share and celebrate their stories and traditions. This chapter covers five different areas that show how culture and heritage, most notably Māori and Pasifika culture, is celebrated and passed on.

Questions such as 'Who are we?', 'How do we represent ourselves?' and 'How are we represented by others?' are raised and dealt with in these various forms of cultural expression. We can see this in the following areas:

- **Film and television — putting New Zealanders in the picture!**
- **Music and song**
- **Sport**
- **Clothing and fashion**
- **Literature and on the stage**

DIVERSITY

Film and television — putting New Zealanders in the picture!

Film

Activity

Pair

1 Complete the following.

a When you think about New Zealand **films**, what film do you think about first? Write it down. See what the person next to you wrote down.

b When you think about New Zealand **television**, what television programme do you think about first? Write it down. See what the person next to you wrote down.

 ISBN: 9780170368117

Since 1898, when the first movie was shot in New Zealand, New Zealanders have been very active in making films and producing film stars. Early New Zealand television programmes showed New Zealanders themselves.

Activity

Independent

2 5 Ws and 1 H.

Complete the 5 Ws and 1 H activity for one of the following early iconic New Zealand productions:

- *Country Calendar*
- *Footrot Flats: The Dog's ~~Tail~~ Tale*

Do some reseach on the production and then fill in each of the balloons with a question. Once you have filled in all of the balloons, answer your questions.

Peter Jackson began his career producing low-budget films in the late 1980s. From the 1990s, the New Zealand film industry began to experience rapid growth due to the establishment of NZ On Air and the international recognition that local films began to receive, mostly for our stunning landscapes. The Alan Duff novel *Once Were Warriors* was made into a film by Māori film-maker Lee Tamahori and showed a violent and brutal New Zealand to the world. It became the highest-grossing film ever released in New Zealand up until that time and met with much controversy due to how it depicted urban Māori. From the early 2000s, New Zealand films began to represent more of Māori and Pasifika culture. In recent years, the film industry has seen the emergence of 'Pollywood' – a Hollywood inspired Polynesian arts scene. South Pacific Pictures, which was responsible for producing a large number of New Zealand films including *Sione's Wedding* and *Whale Rider*, followed other New Zealand film companies such as Screentime and Eyeworks Touchdown by being sold into foreign ownership.

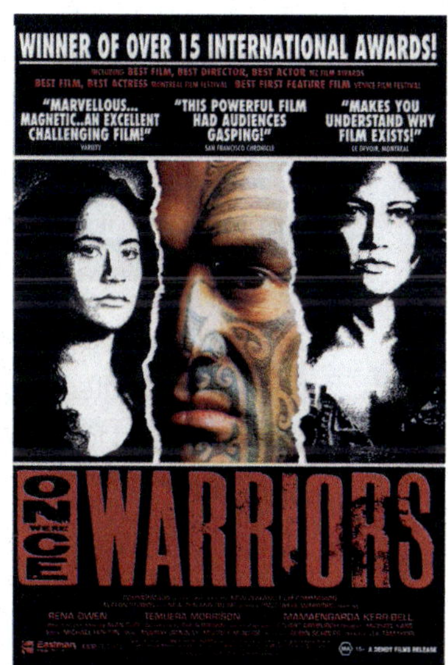

International recognition for a New Zealand film finally happened in 1993 with the Jane Campion-directed film *The Piano* set on the rugged west coast of New Zealand.

Activity

Independent

3 Choose THREE of the films from the list below. For each, find out when the film was released, who directed the film and their background, what culture/cultures are represented, what the film is about and how it was received by the public. See the example below for *Whale Rider*.

- *No. 2*
- *Rain of the Children*
- *Sione's Wedding*
- *Matariki*
- *The Orator*
- *The Dark Horse*
- *River Queen*
- *The Māori Merchant of Venice*
- *Boy*
- *My Wedding and Other Secrets*
- *Sione's 2: Unfinished Business*

Example: *Whale Rider*

When was the film released? The film *Whale Rider* was released in 2002.

Who directed the film and what is their background? The film was directed and written by Niki Caro. Caro was born in Wellington, New Zealand in 1966. She attended Diocesan School for Girls, Auckland and graduated with a BFA from the Elam School of Fine Arts at the University of Auckland. Caro was appointed a Member of the New Zealand Order of Merit for services to the film industry in 2004.

What culture/cultures are represented? Māori culture is the main culture represented.

What is the film about? The film is adapted from the Māori author Witi Ihimaera's novel *The Whale Rider*. Set in a small East Coast New Zealand town, it tells the story of a young Māori girl, Pai, played by Keisha Castle-Hughes, who wants to become the chief of the tribe and challenges tradition.

How was it received by the public? The film received extraordinary worldwide success and won numerous international film festival awards. Keisha Castle-Hughes was nominated for an Academy Award for Best Actress.

Key profile — Oscar Kightley

Samoan-born Oscar Kightley's career began on the stage with a comedy group called *The Naked Samoans*. This group based their comedy on their experiences of growing up culturally misunderstood in Auckland, the world's largest Polynesian city. Success on the stage led Kightley and *The Naked Samoans* to produce the popular animated television comedy series *bro'Town* in 2004. In 2006, he acted in and co-wrote the film *Sione's Wedding*. Since 2006 Kightley has starred in and directed other television programmes, been a radio host and also written a play called *Niu Sila*.

ISBN: 9780170368117

Activities

Independent

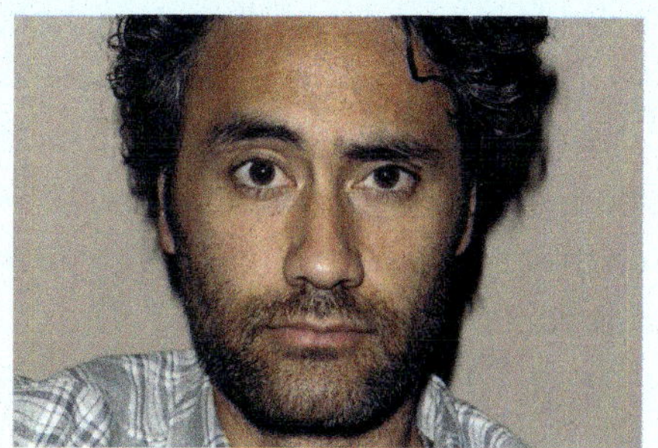

4 Key profile — Taika Waititi.
Copy the structure used for the key profile on Oscar Kightley by putting together your own 'Key profile' for Taika Waititi.

Extra for experts

5 a What impact will the large number of New Zealand film companies being owned outside of New Zealand have on the local film and television industry?

b What is the importance of film funding bodies such as the New Zealand Film Commission, NZ On Air and Creative New Zealand?

c How do films reflect our cultural identity (history and traditions) and our understanding of culture as a whole?

Television

Activity

Pair

6 Complete the following.

a What television programmes do you watch most? Write them down. See what the person next to you wrote down.

b How many of these shows are made in New Zealand?

c Make a list of the different cultural groups that are represented in each of these programmes. Write them down. See what the person next to you wrote down. Discuss.

Television still remains an important cultural **medium** for most New Zealanders since its introduction in 1960. Just like film, television in New Zealand plays an equally important role in reflecting New Zealand's cultural identity. It can help to share and enrich our understanding of culture. The biggest threat to free-to-air television has come from commercially funded privatised television channels. It has meant that channels such as TVNZ6, TVNZ7 and U, which provided cultural and youth-oriented, special interest stories and locally produced documentaries, were shut down as the public funding supply stopped. This has marked a shift away from a public service system.

ISBN: 9780170368117

The ground-breaking television series *Neighbourhood* on TV One explores and celebrates New Zealand's cultural diversity. Each episode is based in a different neighbourhood and is presented by a well-known New Zealander who has a special relationship with that area. The show covers four aspects — creativity, food, politics, and cultural treasures. Search for the series on the internet and find out if a show has been filmed in your neighbourhood.

Asia Downunder, produced by Asia Vision, was funded by NZ On Air to support programmes about and for minority groups. The show ran from 1994 to 2011 until funding ran out.

Activity

Independent

7 Refer to the graph when answering the following questions.

a What is the title of this graph?

b What time period is defined as prime-time?

c How many years in total are covered in this graph?

d The Broadcasting Act 1989 established NZ On Air. What effect did this have on the percentage of prime-time local content? Describe using data from the graph.

e Between 2005 and 2006, three new free-to-air channels were added to the public broadcasting service. They were Prime, Māori TV and C4. Did the inclusion of these three new channels affect the percentage of prime-time local content? Describe using data from the graph.

f Describe, in one sentence, what has happened to the percentage of prime-time local content between 2006 and 2013.

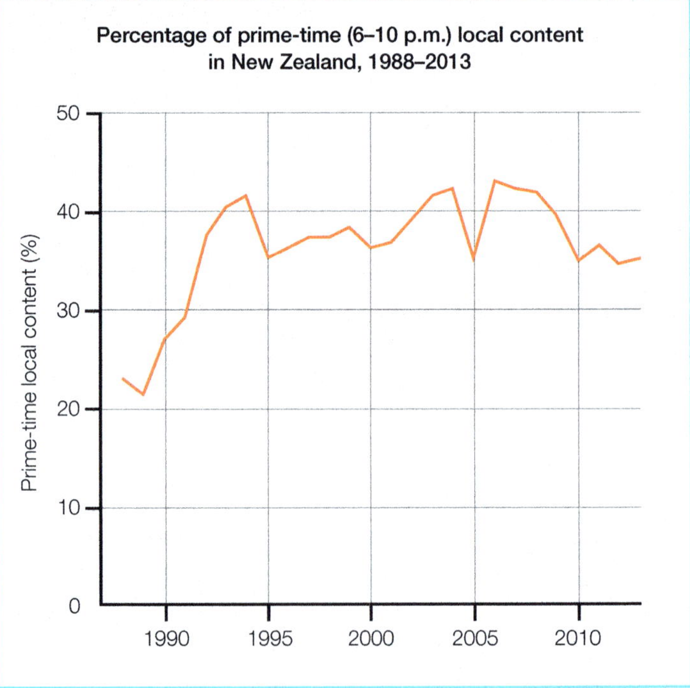

Launched in 2004, the Māori Television channel has become a place for Māori language, culture, custom and history to be promoted and celebrated. It marked a shift away from Māori individuals and groups being seen as just performers and entertainers. It broadcasts mainly in te reo Māori.

DIVERSITY

 ISBN: 9780170368117

Activity

Class

8 Discussion.

NZ On Air is a government broadcast funding agency that invests in diverse local television, radio, music and digital media for New Zealand audiences. More than $80 million a year is spent on local television programmes alone. The primary function of this organisation, as **mandated** under the Broadcasting Act 1989, is to highlight and emphasise cultural identity.

Do you think there is a wide range of broadcasting content available in New Zealand that truly reflects the diversity of Aotearoa? List these programmes and discuss as a class.

Music and song

Music and song are symbolic expressions of shared cultural values. Music reshapes culture and is also shaped by culture. For many cultural groups, songs might be a way to express opinions, as it is a different form of communication to language. Popular New Zealand music covers a diverse range of **genres** and has given a voice to many young people particularly of Pacific Island heritage here in New Zealand.

Music is an area where a distinctive Māori and Pacific identity has emerged. Hip-hop and reggae are two of the most popular genres among youth today. Bands and musicians such as Che Fu, Nesian Mystik, King Kapisi, Scribe, Fat Freddy's Drop, Trinity Roots, Unity Pacific, Ladi6 and many others have enjoyed huge success at home and abroad. These groups all reflect and express their roots, perspectives and cultural pride and heritage through their music.

Search and listen to the song 'Poi E' by the group Patea Māori Club. This number-one hit song, released in 1984, is a uniquely Māori song sung entirely in te reo Māori. The song gained immediate popularity and cult status.

In 2014, Stan Walker wrote and performed a song for the annual Te Wiki o Te Reo Māori (Māori Language Week) entitled 'Aotearoa'. Released 30 years after 'Poi E', it is also sung entirely in te reo Māori.

Nesian Mystik.

Even though the genre of classical music has less popular support at home, New Zealand has produced several very successful composers and international opera singers. These include Dame Kiri Te Kanawa, Jonathan Lemalu and the Samoan group Sol3 Mio.

Sol3 Mio.

CHAPTER 5

In 2000, the Samoan singer King Kapisi released the album *Savage Thoughts*. He raps about his Pacific heritage and immigrant identity as well as issues and challenges relevant to Polynesians living in New Zealand such as the role of Christianity and the church in contemporary Samoan society. In 2002, he launched an urban streetwear clothing label *Overstayer*. He took the name 'overstayer' from the dawn raid era of the 1970s when many Polynesian immigrants were targeted by the Government for deportation.

So what remains New Zealand's biggest-selling and highest-charting single of all time? That award goes to the 1996 song 'How Bizarre' sung by the Otara Millionaires Club (also known as 'OMC'). It still is a global hit song and is one of the most easily recognised New Zealand songs of all time. (If you haven't heard this song before, listen to it!)

Activities

Independent

Arts Access Aotearoa is a charitable trust that works with individuals and groups who wish to participate and contribute to the arts in New Zealand. They encourage refugee and migrant groups to celebrate their own cultures.

9 Go to the Arts Access Aotearoa website and find some case studies of individuals and groups who have received funding to contribute to the arts. Choose one case study and write a two to three-paragraph summary on the background, objectives, challenges and achievements.

Pair

10 **a** Make a list all the *genres* of music you know of. Compare your list with the person next to you and add any others.

b Choose one musical genre from your list. Find out where this music genre originated, when it became established in New Zealand and some of the main influences on this genre.

c Make a list all of the New Zealand *bands and musicians* you know of. Compare your list with the person next to you and add any others.

d Choose one of the bands or musicians from your list. Find out the names of the members, where they are from, how long they have been singing for and what are some of the issues they sing about.

ISBN: 9780170368117

Sport

Many sports in New Zealand today reflect the country's British heritage such as rugby, cricket, football/soccer and golf. You only need to watch a national sports team play, whether it's the All Blacks, Silver Ferns, Tall Blacks or the New Zealand Rugby League team, along with many sports, to see the significant impact that cultural diversity has had on New Zealand's sporting success.

Activities

Pair

11 a Make a list of all of the sports that are played at your school in summer and in winter.

b What sports are played in other parts of the country that are not played at your school? Why?

c Research (by percentage of participation) the THREE most popular sports in New Zealand.

d Why is sport an important part of New Zealand's identity?

Independent

12 a Choose one of the national sports teams from the list below or another if you want. Using the internet, research the current team. Make a list of all of the members of that team. Next to their names, write down their ethnicity. Construct a pie chart of your results. Make sure to include a title and a key. (Refer to Skill 4: Drawing a Pie Chart, page 6.)

Choose from:

Rugby — All Blacks
Cricket — Black Caps
Rugby League — the Kiwis.
Netball — Silver Ferns
Basketball — Tall Blacks

b Compare your pie chart on a national sporting team's ethnicity with someone else in your class who researched a different team to you. What conclusions can you draw about the ethnic diversity of your chosen national sporting team?

ISBN: 9780170368117

New Zealand firsts

Shaun Johnson is a professional rugby league player who currently plays for the New Zealand Warriors and the Kiwis. He is the first New Zealand international representative of Laotian ancestry, as his mother is from Laos, a country in South-East Asia.

What other New Zealand firsts can you think of?

A revival in traditional Maori sport and games

In recent decades, there has been an effort to revive many traditional Māori sports and games that were played before Europeans arrived in New Zealand. These include *kī-o-rahi*, *poi rākau*, *whakatere waka* (waka racing) and *kite flying* (at Matariki festivals).

Activities

Independent

13 There are four Maori sports and games listed in the paragraph above. For each, find an image of the sport or game and write at least one paragraph describing how the sport or game is traditionally played, what the rules are and what equipment is used.

14 Write a statement on what you have learned about sport and cultural identity in New Zealand.

Clothing and fashion

Ethnic and national costumes reflect cultures. What people wear can highlight cultural differences and help to reveal their cultural identity. People might wear ethnic or national dress on special occasions.

Until the 1980s, much of New Zealand's fashion design was heavily influenced by international trends. However, since the mid-1990s, more and more designers in the fields of graphic, jewellery and clothing design have started using Māori, Polynesian and New Zealand influences in their work. The success of local labels at overseas fashion weeks has raised the profile of fashion in New Zealand.

Style Pasifika was an annual and iconic showcase of music, dance and cultural performances. It also included the Style Pasifika Fashion Awards, which had several categories, one of which was for traditionally inspired designs. Style Pasifika ran for 17 years from 1995 to 2011.

 ISBN: 9780170368117

Activities

Pair

15 Below is a list of traditional items of ethnic and national clothing on the left and countries on the right. Match up the clothing with the country it is from.

Abayat	South Korea
Cheongsam	Tonga
Kimono	Mexico
Sari	Germany
Jellabiya	Greece
Fustanella	Scotland
Lederhosen	Japan
Hanbok	India
Puletasi	China
Charro	Oman
Tupenu	Samoa
Kilt	Egypt

16 New Zealand does not have a specific national dress. Come up with three possible options for what it could be.

Independent

17 Find the names of some well-known Māori and Pacific Island fashion designers in New Zealand. What do they design? What influences come through in their work?

Literature and on the stage

Activity

Group

18 Think, pair, share!

Think: Create a T-chart. On the left side, write down all of the New Zealand stage actors and live comedians that you can think of. On the right side, write down all of the writers, poets and playwrights that you can think of.

Pair: Discuss your T-chart with the person next to you. Share your answers with each other. Add any new names to your T-chart.

Share: In groups of three or four, share your T-charts. Add any new names to your T-chart.

CHAPTER 5

There has been a long and proud tradition of challenging audiences with confronting issues such as talking about the migrant experience. In 1985, *The Penguin Book of New Zealand Verse* published, for the first time, poetry in te reo Māori. This showed the changing values of the time and allowed many other writers, poets and actors from Māori culture and from **marginalised** cultural backgrounds to start to create and perform drawing on their own cultural backgrounds for inspiration.

Huia Publishers was set up in 1991 to promote Māori writers. It publishes work in both English and te reo Māori.

Alistair Te Ariki Campbell was born in Rarotonga and is a famous New Zealand Pacific Island novelist, poet and playwright. At university in New Zealand he became good friends with James K. Baxter, another well-known New Zealand poet. Campbell published more than 20 volumes of poetry, which gave a profound insight into the problems that faced Polynesians in the face of British colonisation.

Albert Wendt is a Samoan poet, painter and writer. He is internationally recognised as a leader of New Zealand and Pacific literature since the 1970s. He became one of the first Samoan and Pacific Island professors in New Zealand. He won the 1980 New Zealand Book Award for his book *Leaves of the Banyan Tree*.

Witi Ihimaera is one of the most prominent Māori writers in New Zealand. He has written numerous short stories and novels including *Yellow Brick Road*, *Woman Far Walking* and *The Whale Rider*, which was turned into a film. Ihimaera's books show aspects of Māori culture in modern New Zealand and reveal problems within contemporary Māori society.

Karlo Mila-Schaaf is of Tongan, Samoan and European descent. Her first collection of poems, *Dream Fish Floating*, published by Huia Publishers, won the 2006 New Zealand Book Award for Best First Book of Poetry. Mila-Schaaf completed a PhD in Sociology, which looked at culture, identities and wellbeing among New Zealand-born Pacific Islanders.

John Pule is a New Zealand Niuean poet, artist and novelist. The topic of his work is often focused on issues to do with Christianity, migration and colonialism. He has also helped to revive the traditional Polynesian art form of tapa cloth painting.

 ISBN: 9780170368117

Activity

Independent

19 Above are five short key profiles looking at the area of **literature**. Write five more short key profiles on the following influential people and groups that have helped to shape the New Zealand **stage**.

- Billy T. James
- Madeleine Sami (pictured)
- The Laughing Samoans
- Lynda Chanwai-Earle
- Jacob Rajan

Time to recap

1 What is the most significant thing you have learned in this chapter? Why?

2 'The Muddiest Point'. Write down which part of this chapter was difficult to understand. Compare what you wrote down with someone else. Find someone in the class who can explain it to you.

CHAPTER 5

ISBN: 9780170368117

Air New Zealand arrivals
Koru Lounge
Public
Pick up

6

CHANGE AND CHALLENGES AHEAD

'I am a citizen, not of Athens or Greece, but of the world.'

– Socrates

Learning intentions

After studying this chapter you should understand that:

- cultures adapt and change and that this has consequences for society.

Useful words

superdiverse — very culturally diverse.

globalisation — the process of cultures and people interacting around the world, often through trade.

extinct — having died out, for ever.

Dealing with change

New Zealand now has more ethnicities than the world has countries. This is why people have started calling New Zealand a **superdiverse** country. By 2030, New Zealand's population is expected to reach five million. Most of that growth will be due to migrants from other countries immigrating to New Zealand. Never before has New Zealand had such a large number of people living here that were born overseas. This also means that the number of perspectives on a wide range of social and cultural issues is ever increasing.

4,442,100
New Zealand population 2013 census

541,300
Asian population

+12% Proportion of people who identified with at least one Asian ethnicity in 2003

In 2015, The Superdiversity Stocktake was launched by the Superdiversity Centre. It marked the first time that in-depth research and forecasting had been done on the consequences of New Zealand's ethnic superdiversity for business, government and people in the future. The 'Cultural Bridge' service was also launched in 2015 as a joint venture between the Superdiversity Centre and NZME (New Zealand Media and Entertainment).

Activities

Independent

1 Go to www.culturalbridge.co.nz and make a list of the services they offer.

2 Who will be interested in using this service?

Pair

3 Thinking about a current issue.

Choose ONE of the following social or cultural issues (or another that you may know of) that has a range of perspectives, beliefs and values. For example: laws on smacking, same-sex marriage, organ donation, abortion, how people treat the environment, stem-cell research.

Identify a range of different cultural perspectives on the social or cultural issue. Place all of these on a **continuum** (see Chapter 3 for an explanation of a continuum).

Include a justification for where you have placed the different perspectives and why.

ISBN: 9780170368117

According to the 2013 New Zealand census figures, a massive 25 percent of people living in New Zealand today were born overseas. England, China and India are the three most common countries of birth for overseas-born people living in New Zealand. That change is already visible in the city of Auckland, where more than half a million people were born overseas. Auckland city is now more multicultural than Sydney or London, with over 200 ethnicities calling Auckland home. The most rapid growth in Auckland has been in the city's Asian population, with one in four Aucklanders now of Asian ethnicity; this is predicted to be one in three by the early 2020s. The Asian population is also now larger than Māori and Pasifika populations combined.

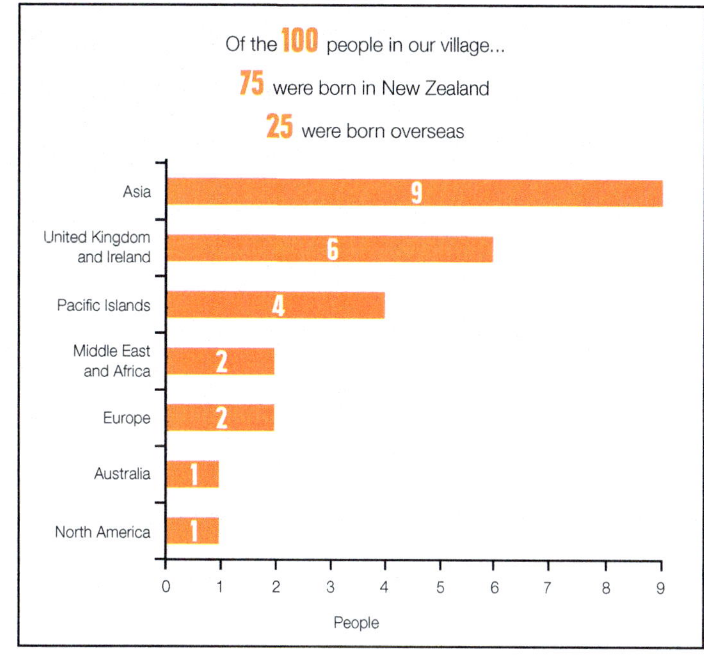

Activities

Independent

4 On the internet, search for 'Asia New Zealand Foundation' and answer the following questions.

- a When was this organisation set up?
- b What are some areas that they support?
- c Give an example of an event or festival that they help to organise.
- d What are some opportunities they give to students?

5 Statistical graphics.

Statistical graphics are used to visualise complex data. The THREE statistical graphics on page 86 display data from the 2013 New Zealand Census for the cities of Auckland, Wellington and Christchurch.

Spend some time looking at each of these three statistical graphics. Try to understand the data that they display. Complete the following questions **for each of the three graphics**:

- a What four ethnic groups are included in the graphic?
- b What was the population of the city in 1996?
- c What was the population of the city in 2013?
- d What is the projected population of the city in 2038?
- e In 1996, what ethnic group is the **biggest**? Use specific data in your answer (e.g. the percentage).
- f In 1996, what ethnic group is the **smallest**? Use specific data in your answer (e.g. the percentage).
- g In 2013, what ethnic group is the **biggest**? Use specific data in your answer (e.g. the percentage).
- h In 2013, what ethnic group is the **smallest**? Use specific data in your answer (e.g. the percentage).

i What ethnic group has **increased** the most between 1996 and 2013? Use specific data in your answer (e.g. the percentage). Provide a possible reason for this increase.

j What ethnic group has **decreased** the most between 1996 and 2013? Use specific data in your answer (e.g. the percentage). Provide a possible reason for this increase.

k Based on the projection in 2038 by Statistics New Zealand, rank the four ethnic groups from largest to smallest. Use specific data in your answer (e.g. the percentage).

l Brainstorm some potential positive and negative consequences of this change in the ethnic population for this city in 2038.

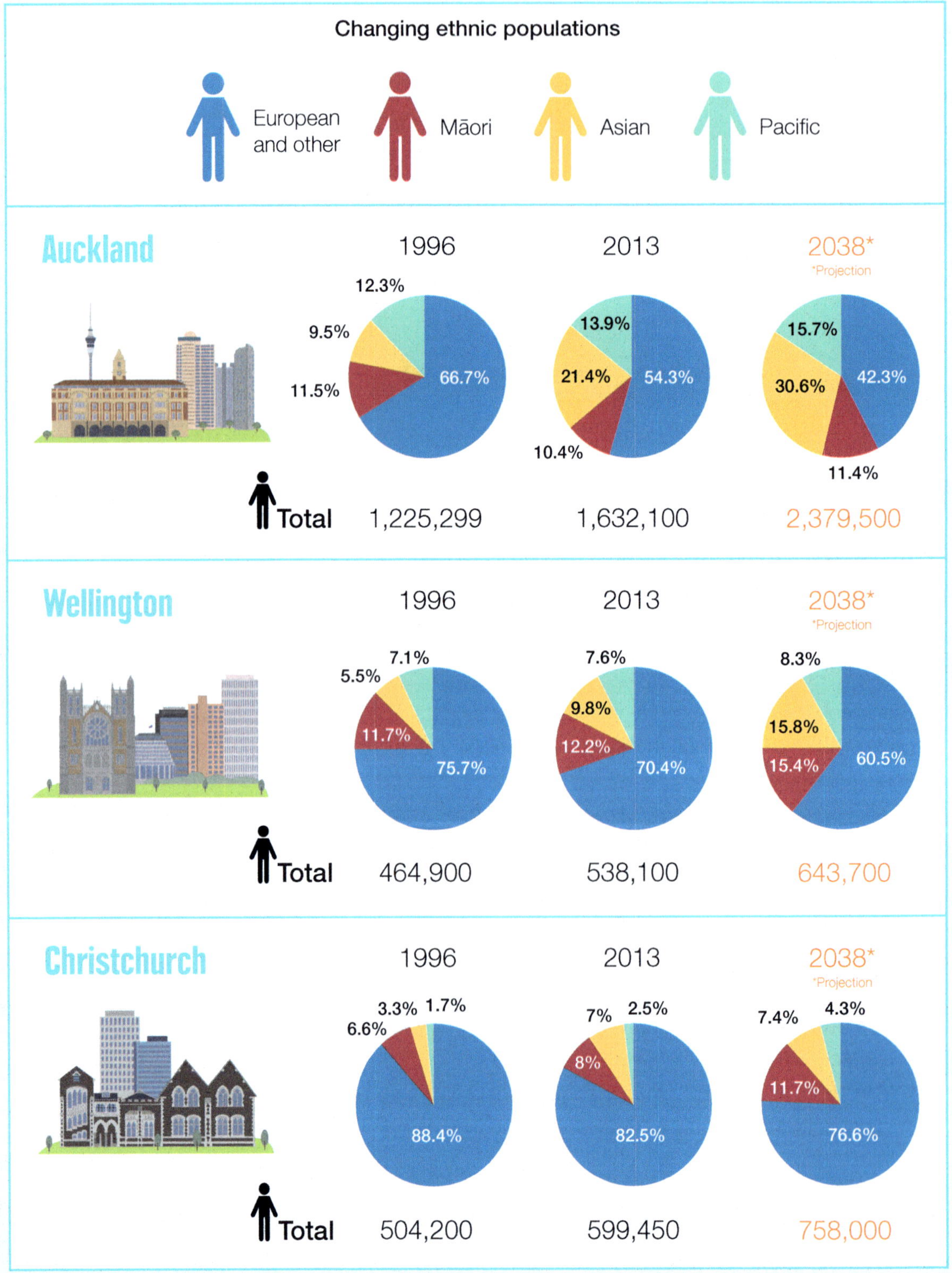

 ISBN: 9780170368117

Managing migration

Migration is one of the key challenges that faces New Zealand today and into the future. This raises the question of who we are and how we see ourselves in the world. There is pressure on the New Zealand Government to accept higher immigration numbers as well as more skilled and well-educated migrants.

Activities

Pair

6 PMI — Plus, Minus, Interesting.
Try to write down THREE of each.

- What are the positive (**P**lus) things about migration?
- What are the negative (**M**inus) things about migration?
- What is interesting (**I**nteresting) about migration?

Class

7 As a class, write a letter to your local Member of Parliament (MP), with a list of suggestions about what the New Zealand Government could do to help new immigrants to settle in our country.

Extra for experts

8 Can the Auckland housing crisis be blamed on immigration to Auckland? Explain.

Since the Christchurch earthquake of 2011, there has been a large demand for skilled migrants to go to Christchurch to help with the $40 billion rebuild of the city. However, in general, many provincial New Zealand towns and communities are not growing and are not attracting new migrants.

CHAPTER 6

ISBN: 9780170368117

Activities

Independent

9 Some small communities like the ones mentioned on the previous page, according to the New Zealand Institute of Economic Research (NZIER) economist Shamubeel Eaqub, have become 'zombie towns'. Complete the following.

- **a** What does the NZIER do?
- **b** What does Eaqub mean by the phrase 'zombie towns'?
- **c** Find some examples of modern-day 'zombie towns' in New Zealand.

10 Do you agree or disagree with the following statement? Why?
'Our colonial connection to the United Kingdom as a European or Western country is gone.'

11 Comparing New Zealand's cultural diversity with another country.

- **a** Compare New Zealand's changing cultural diversity with what is happening in Australia or a country in the Pacific, for example Fiji. Discuss in at least two or three paragraphs.
- **b** Use a Venn diagram (see Chapter 4) to describe *similarities* and *differences* between the changing cultural diversity in New Zealand and in the country you have chosen, using specific evidence.

Threats to cultural diversity

The world today is becoming increasingly globalised. With increased **globalisation** of trade and technology, New Zealand is now much more connected to the Asia/Pacific and Oceanic region than it used to be. New information and communication technologies have become real threats to cultural diversity. Fewer and fewer cultural groups are having any real say in the direction and future of modern-day society. Thousands of languages spoken around the world are under threat. One language is becoming extinct every two weeks. It is estimated that around half of the world's 7000 languages will be **extinct** or on the verge of extinction by the end of this century.

Activity

Independent

12 Answer the following.

- **a** Why are many of the world's languages under threat of extinction?
- **b** Why should we be worried about the loss of language?

ISBN: 9780170368117

Activities

Class

13 Discussion.
Do you think that cultural rights of many cultural groups are being ignored and undermined in today's society?

Extra for experts

14 a The opposite of cultural diversity is cultural uniformity. Should we encourage *cultural uniformity* or *cultural diversity*? Explain.

b Analyse the potential impact of the internet and globalisation on cultural diversity in the future.

Challenges ahead: The three Ps – *Protecting, Preserving* and *Promoting* cultural diversity

The United Nations named 2002 the Year for Cultural Heritage. Two important annual days have been established to help people understand the value of cultural diversity, to eliminate racial discrimination and to help people learn how to live together in peace and harmony:

21 March – Race Relations Day in New Zealand. The 2015 theme was 'Big change starts small'. Each year students can enter a Race Unity speech competition.

21 May – World Day for Cultural Diversity. In 2011, a Facebook community page was set up entitled 'Do One Thing for Diversity and Inclusion'. It encourages people and organisations from around the world to take action to support diversity.

Ten stories from around the world

Cherry Tree by Ruskin Bond
Boundless Grace by Mary Hoffman and Caroline Binch
Arctic Son by Jean Craighead George
Galimoto by Karen Lynn Williams
Waiting for the Biblioburro by Monica Brown
Rechenka's Eggs by Patricia Polacco
Are We There Yet? A Journey Around Australia by Alison Lester
Linnea in Monet's Garden by Cristina Bjork and Lena Anderson
The White Nights of Ramadan by Maha Addasi
Ruby's Wish by Shirin Yim Bridges

CHAPTER 6

ISBN: 9780170368117

Activities

Independent

15 **a** Find out where the 10 stories from around the world are set.

b Choose one of the stories that you can get out from your school or local library. Complete the following questions.

- **i** What is the title of the book?
- **ii** Who wrote the book?
- **iii** Who illustrated the book?
- **iv** Where is the story set?
- **v** Describe the main characters.
- **vi** Describe the plot (that is, what happens).
- **vii** What main ideas/themes does the author explore?
- **viii** What have you learned from this story?

Pair

16 **a** For each of the three Ps below, do the following:
Write a ONE-paragraph explanation of what it means and why it is important.

- *Protecting* cultural diversity
- *Preserving* cultural diversity
- *Promoting* cultural diversity

b Find a specific example in New Zealand (that has not been covered in this book) that shows what a group or organisation is doing for one of these.

In the future

Any society faces challenges when people and groups from diverse cultures live side by side. This is now a reality for almost every country or region in the world. Many regions have been in conflict for a long time as a result of cultural differences, misunderstandings and a lack of tolerance. People must not lose sight of the common heritage that is shared. In New Zealand we have the opportunity to look at the changes and challenges that come from being a superdiverse country and embrace it.

Cultural diversity is not something that is going to go away tomorrow. It is the common heritage for all humanity. New Zealand is one of the most peaceful nations in the world. It's up to all New Zealanders to ensure this is a legacy we leave for future generations.

 ISBN: 9780170368117

Activities

Pair

17 Looking to the future: 'If' and 'then'.

Come up with a series of 'If' scenarios and link them with a 'then' possible outcome for the future of cultural diversity in New Zealand.

For example: *If* New Zealand doesn't allow more refugees to settle here, *then* the refugees will have nowhere else to go.

Class

18 Find an image that for you best reflects New Zealand's cultural diversity.

Explain your image to the class saying why you chose this image, what it shows and why, for you, it best reflects New Zealand's cultural diversity.

Time to recap

1 What is the most significant thing you have learned in this chapter? Why?

2 'The Muddiest Point'. Write down which part of this chapter was difficult to understand. Compare what you wrote down with someone else. Find someone in the class who can explain it to you.

CHAPTER 6

1

CARRYING OUT A SOCIAL INQUIRY

'Let's stop believing that our differences make us superior or inferior to one another.'

— #NZDiversity

There are many challenges that come from the increasing diversity of cultures in New Zealand. Some examples of these challenges might include the different perspectives, beliefs and values that individuals and groups have about the following significant social and cultural issues:

- laws on smacking
- same-sex marriage
- organ donation
- abortion
- how people treat the environment
- stem-cell research.

Using the social inquiry model (there is an example in this chapter), you are able to ask questions, find information, and examine the background and consequences of significant social and cultural issues and events. You are able to explore different values and perspectives relating to these issues and develop understandings about the ways people respond and make decisions. Lastly, you will get the opportunity to reflect and evaluate on the social inquiry that you have undertaken.

Things to consider before you start your social inquiry

1 **What will be the topic/focus of my social inquiry and what are the key concepts? (It should be related to a significant social or cultural issue.)**

2 **Where will I get information from?**

- Internet, school and local library, TV, documentaries, textbooks and handouts from your teacher, newspapers, magazines.

3 **Using the internet (See Skill 6: Using the Internet, page 7)**

Some websites are better than others and being able to know the difference is an essential skill to develop. It will also help you to decide if a source is **useful** and **reliable**. To do this, ask yourself the following:

- Who made the website?
- What is the source of the information?

ISBN: 9780170368117

- Can the website be edited by anyone? Websites like wikipedia.org are online encyclopaedias that can be added to and altered by anyone. Poor writing or spelling mistakes are indications that the website has not been written by experts.
- Does the information on the website support only one viewpoint? This might help you to work out if there is bias, or prejudice, in the information you have accessed.

4 **Making a time management plan**

A time management plan will help you when carrying out your social inquiry. Your teacher will help you set deadlines for the four milestones:

- Confirming your focus of learning
- Finding information and deciding on the key concepts
- Completing the work
- Considering 'So what?', 'What now?'

5 **Keeping an inquiry journal**

This is a good way of recording what you have done throughout your social inquiry. This is called self-reflection. In your journal you can record not only the milestones you have reached but also your thoughts and feelings about your social inquiry. You can record the things that you would like to find out more about in the future. At the end of your inquiry you will be able to look back through your inquiry journal when writing your evaluation. This will make it easier for you to comment on what went well and what you might do differently next time.

6 **How will I communicate what I have learned during my social inquiry?**

Your teacher will tell you how they would like you to present your findings. This might be as a poster, a speech, a PowerPoint or Prezi, a social action, or in some other format.

On the next page is a social inquiry model example. The issue is the traditional prayer used to open daily sittings of New Zealand's Parliament.

CHAPTER 7

Social Inquiry Model Example

Focusing of learning/topic
In 2014, New Zealand Parliament's Speaker David Carter rejected a move by MPs to change the traditional daily prayer.

Key concepts
Beliefs, identity, diversity, traditions, customs, rights, groups.

Conceptual understandings
Understand how cultural practices vary but reflect similar purposes.
(Level 3 AO)

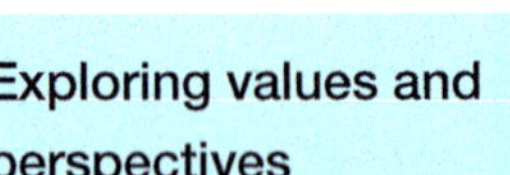

Exploring values and perspectives

- What are the beliefs and values of people who have different perspectives about this issue?
- Has New Zealand society and its institutions allowed for diverse faiths and practices to be exercised?
- Why is this issue important?

Reflecting and evaluating.

- Are the sources we have used balanced, **useful** and **reliable**?
- What more do we need to know and find out?
- Do we understand the different opinions and perspectives on this issue?

Finding out information

- What is the traditional prayer that the Speaker uses to open daily sittings of Parliament, and for how many years has it been used?
- What religious references are contained in the prayer?
- How much support was there from MPs for a change to the daily traditional prayer?
- What is the public's opinion on this issue?
- What are some of the actual or potential problems that this issue has raised?

Considering responses and decisions

- In what ways can people's religious beliefs and practices lead to concern, difficulty, misunderstanding or conflict between different cultural groups in a society?
- What could the New Zealand Government do to resolve this issue?

Further inquiry for future learning

- So what does this mean for me/others?
  - What implications does the decision by the Speaker have for us, others, and the community?
- Now what might be done about it?
  - What steps in our learning could we take next?
  - What can we do as an individual, as a class or as a school?

 ISBN: 9780170368117